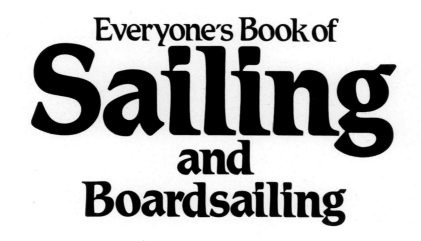

Everyone's Book of
Sailing
and
Boardsailing

Everyone's Book of
Sailing
and
Boardsailing

Bob Māthias
Bob Bond

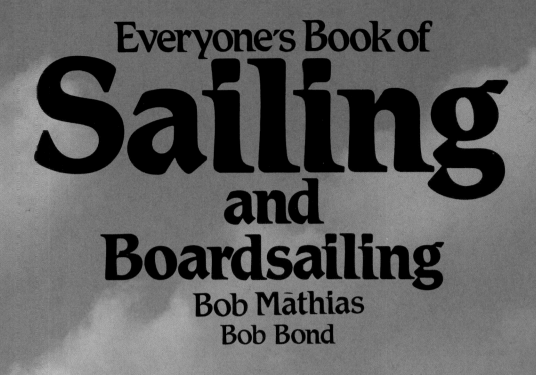

Photographic acknowledgments
Agence Vandystadt – Ch. Petit-Wind 80 top; Beken of Cowes 10-11, 12, 14 top left, 14 top right, 14 bottom left, 14 bottom right, 15, 24, 28, 31, 42, 66; Alastair Black, Lee-on-Solent 16-17; Bob Bond 68-69, 78; Colour Library International, London 6-7, 9, 19; David Eberlin 70, 73, 74 top, 74-75, 77 top right, 77 top centre, 77 bottom centre, 77 bottom, 79; Hamlyn Group Picture Library 27 top, 27 bottom, 35, 37 62, 63, 64 top, 64 bottom; Bob Mathias 34; Photosport Magazine – D. Edmund Jones 80 bottom; Barry Pickthall, Arundel 33, 40-41, 49, 50; Spectrum Colour Library, London 8; George Taylor, Poole 20, 29, 44, 5 57, 60; John Watney, London 23, 30, 47, 52, 53, 55, 56, 58; G. Way 76, 77 left.

Front cover: Colour Library International
Back cover: Tony Taylor
Endpapers: Nigel Snowdon and Associates
Contents spread: Agence Vandystadt, Paris
Line illustrations by Bob Mathias

Contents

Introduction to Sailing

The attraction of sailing is that it is all things to all men. Square-jawed, clean-faced uniformed crews race expensively and seriously in finely tuned boats. Constructed from space-age materials, they are worth their weight in gold (well, almost). Whole families, clad from head to foot in bright yellow and orange, flood on to the seas in small tubby boats bulging with all the comforts of home. Others, more spartan, hanker for the past; despising anything remotely connected with the twentieth century. Tarry-sweatered, sea-booted and usually unshaven, they gaze tirelessly into the far distance seeking some long-forgotten horizon. I even know of one sailor who doesn't sail. His time is spent building his dream boat. It is a strange craft, and he intends to circle the world in it. But he will build forever and the boat will never be finished.

For me sailing is many things. It is the joy of being in command of a well-found, tidy boat free on the sea and capable of going anywhere the wind, and my courage, will take it. It is the peace of an early mist-morning start to a voyage, when one seems to be the only person awake in the world. It is the heightened experience of facing the unknown when thrashing along in a strong breeze on a night so black that there is no horizon, when all that can be seen are the white crests of the waves rushing under the stern. It is the satisfaction felt after a long passage when the boat is finally berthed and all is snug and well secured, when everything on the boat has done its job well and your judgment has proved to be sound.

No one can ever sit back and say, 'I know all there is to know about sailing.' It is more than just a sport, it is a way of life and, like life, one never stops learning. It is my hope that what lessons I have learnt will help some to improve their skills and give others an introduction to this most enjoyable of pastimes.

One thing that cannot be stressed enough is that there is a right way and a wrong way to do all things. The sea does not tolerate fools and a thoughtless action or careless error of judgment can have dire results. Whichever way your interest is directed this fact must not be ignored. A lot of care and a little forethought, and above all patience, can make the difference between a pleasant trouble-free trip and a disaster for both yourself and others. Learn from your mistakes but remember that some mistakes can never be repeated.

Bob Mathias

Xargo III, an ocean racing ketch, reaches along in a soldier's wind.

How a Boat Works

The sailors' brown backs glistened in the early morning sun as they heaved on the thick lines. Slowly they hauled the long heavy lateen spar to the top of the short mast. The mist had lifted and a soft breeze rustled the reeds along the bank. The huge flax sail took shape as it slowly filled and the dhow quietly moved, its low hull gliding out on to the sun-rippled waters of the Nile. The breeze came from slightly ahead and the boat moved across the water smoothly and silently.

This was how it was in ancient Egypt and how it remains to this day in many parts of the Near and Far East. Man has known how to harness the wind to his own ends for centuries and, in small boats, ply his trade on the rivers and seas of the world.

How does a boat use the wind? The dhow mentioned above was one of the earliest craft built with not only the ability to sail freely before the wind, that is with the wind coming from astern and pushing it along, but also with the great advantage of being able to sail into the wind – to sail in the direction from which the wind was coming. It did this by setting a triangular sail along the fore-and-aft line of the hull.

The dhow with its tall lateen sail can make way against the prevailing wind.

For some obscure, illogical reason the dhow's design concepts and inherent flexibility were shelved and placed in nautical hibernation for centuries. Man continued to develop his sailing activities, but along lines which seemingly ignored this critical discovery. He concentrated only on what we know today as *square rig*.

Right: A replica of Sir Francis Drake's square-rigged ship the *Golden Hind*.

Overleaf: The three-masted training ship *Christian Radich* under full sail. She flies the courtesy ensign of Great Britain as she sails in U.K. waters.

The Roman, Spanish, Portuguese, French and English mariners all hoisted a square sail, setting it at right angles to the line of the hull and running before the following wind. In the cold waters of the North the Vikings launched their long open boats, and under square sails drove into the chill unknown waters of the Arctic to sail on until they trod the soil of the Americas. If the wind happened to be against them they were forced to wait until it blew once more in their favour.

Such unpredictability is incredible to contemplate. How many voyages of discovery failed – or would have succeeded earlier, if marine development had taken a different direction. How many sea battles recorded in history would have been won instead of lost. And how many sailors would have been saved from drowning if their ships could have sailed into the wind and prevented them being driven ashore and wrecked.

THE GOLDEN AGE

With experience, and a greater knowledge and understanding of the prevailing winds encircling the globe, marine architects built bigger and bigger square-rigged ships. Their captains established major trade routes and left few parts of the world unexplored.

Columbus sailed his tiny overcrowded carrack *Santa Maria* from Spain in 1492 in search of a route to the East Indies, and mistakenly discovered the West Indies. Later, in 1519, the Portuguese navigator Magellan took a small fleet of five ships and, with only one surviving, the *Victoria*, circumnavigated the world for the first time. And on a raw London morning in 1768 Captain James Cook departed in a converted coal ship, the *Endeavour*, to circle the world and discover the great land mass of Australia.

This was the Golden Age of Sail, but few of these magnificent craft have survived to the present day. A few of the later craft are preserved, to remind us of more intrepid times. The *Cutty Sark*, one of the last great tea clippers, lies in permanent dock at Greenwich, England. She gained her fame racing the sixteen thousand miles from the Far East to London. Nelson's famous flagship *Victory* rests in Portsmouth, a memorial to her hundreds of crewmen who struggled to keep her sailing in the right direction at Trafalgar. In Stockholm the *Vasa* has been lifted bodily from the mud of the sound where she sank on her maiden voyage in 1628. After more than three hundred years she remains virtually undamaged.

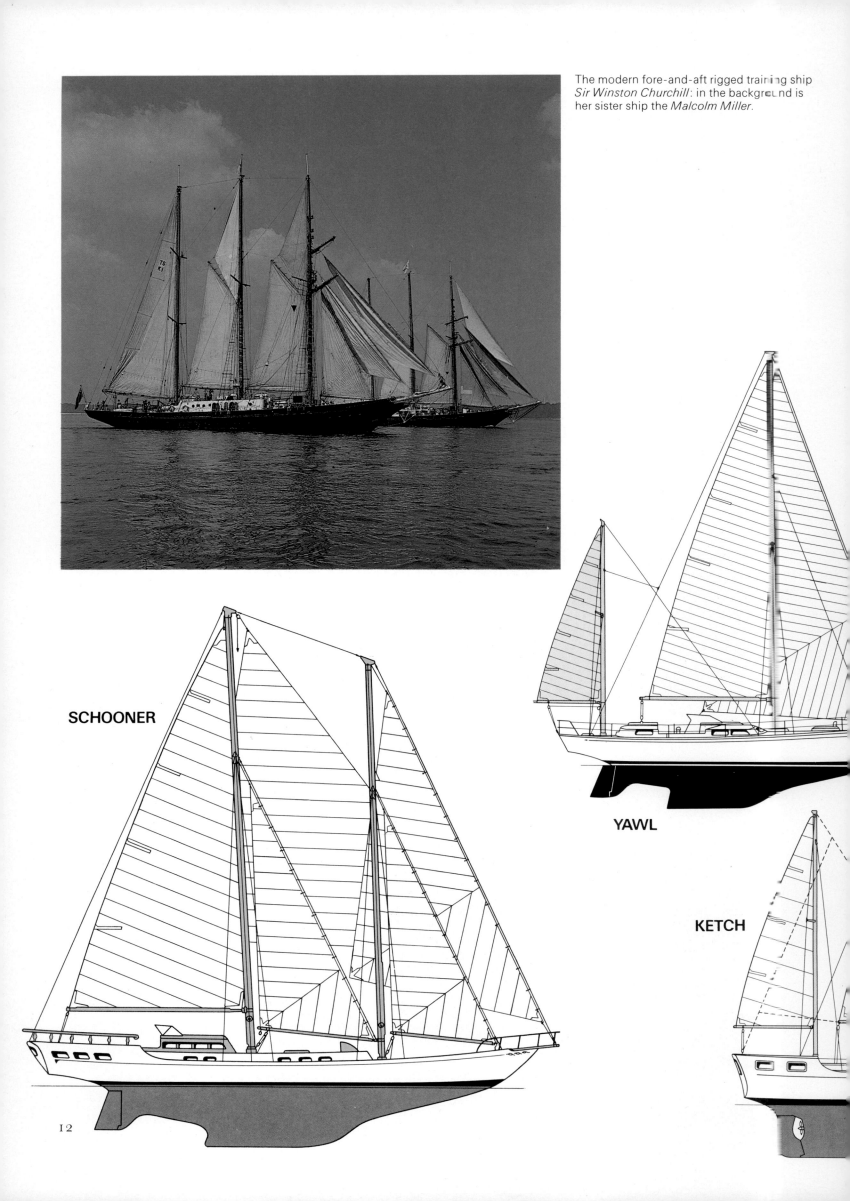

The modern fore-and-aft rigged training ship *Sir Winston Churchill*: in the background is her sister ship the *Malcolm Miller*.

SCHOONER

YAWL

KETCH

12

Progress towards fore-and-aft rig was slow, but when its merits were rediscovered it soon almost totally replaced the use of square rig. Today this great age is reflected only in the continued use of the square-rigged 'Tall Ships', for training the young people of all nations in the ways of the sea.

FORE-AND-AFT RIG

The idea of setting a sail in a line from fore and aft was adopted quickly and inventively. Marine architects devised all manner of permutations to exploit its potential. Today, with sailing almost exclusively a leisure activity, the rig has been refined down to five basic forms. In order of reverse efficiency against the wind they are the schooner, ketch, yawl, cutter and sloop.

The schooner rig comprises a two-masted vessel with the aft, or rear, mast being the taller of the two. The ketch rig also consists of two masts but the forward, or main mast, is the taller of the two; the aft mast is referred to as the mizzen mast. A yawl is very similar to a ketch but the mizzen mast is stepped (placed) aft of the rudder post whereas on a ketch it is positioned forward of the rudder post. The cutter carries a single mast but is rigged with a bowsprit, a short spar set horizontally protruding from its bow. The bowsprit extends the overall length of the boat and enables it to set two headsails forward of the mast. The most popular and unquestionably the most efficient of the five main rigs is the sloop. It has a single mast with a mainsail set on a boom aft and a single headsail, loose-footed (without a boom), forward. Both sails are now invariably triangular and the accepted term for this type of craft is the Bermudan sloop.

CUTTER

SLOOP

Top left: The schooner *La Goleta* is a good example of amalgamated rigs. Basically she is cutter rigged with a gaff staysail but she also carries a Bermudian mainsail.

Top right: A ketch of the Endurance Class.

The sloop's potentially superior sailing performance against the wind is a compound of many factors. These include hull size and shape, displacement, the wind resistance of the superstructure, the materials of construction and the vessel's weight, the relative area of sail to mast height and her bow entry into the water – all these factors need to be right if the vessel is to acquit herself well.

GAFF RIG

Although fore-and-aft rig became the order of the day the square shape of the sail remained in use for a considerable time. However, the outer corner of a square mainsail, the one furthest from the mast, requires support and so a second boom was hoisted to add the necessary stability. This extra boom was called a gaff.

Initially the odd triangular space left above the gaff and behind the mast was filled with a small topsail but about the turn of the century the two sails were amalgamated into one. This dispensed with the need for the gaff and the modern triangular mainsail came into being.

Above left: A graceful example of a yawl – the French yacht *Latifa*

Above right: A German cruising sloop rigged as a cutter.

Right: A modern racing sloop flying two spinnakers to catch the light winds.

Above: The complexities of a typical gaff-rigged mast showing the shrouds and halyard arrangements.

Left: Old gaffers enjoying a leisurely day's racing.

Gaff rig can be adapted to suit any of the five categories mentioned, so you can have a gaff schooner or a gaff sloop. Many old gaff-rigged craft are still in commission and, despite being somewhat cumbersome and old-fashioned, are still very popular for leisurely cruising.

HULL SHAPE

The hull can be loosely divided into three areas: the foredeck, the area from the stem running back to the coachroof or cabin; the midships section, the area occupied by the cabin and accommodation, and the cockpit, the control centre of the boat where the helmsman sits to steer the boat and watch the sails. But to examine a hull closely it is useful to know how a vessel is measured.

There are four basic statistics which determine the shape of a boat's hull. The greatest (often regarded as the most prestigious) is the *Length Over All* (abbreviated to LOA). This is the total length of the boat measured at deck level from stem to stern. Her *Load Waterline Length* (LWL) is her length on the water from bow to stern with the boat floating at rest. The width of the hull at its widest part is referred to as the *beam*, and lastly the depth of water occupied by the hull is the *draught*.

There is a fifth dimension which is seldom quoted but does nevertheless affect the sailing performance of a boat. This is the *freeboard*, which is the distance between the water level and the height of the deck at its lowest point. Too much freeboard will create wind resistance causing the boat to drift sideways – a great disadvantage when manoeuvring in a crowded anchorage. Too little freeboard and the boat will undoubtedly be very wet under sail as she heels over in the wind.

It is a fairly good guide when looking at a hull to indulge in the highly non-scientific philosophy of the grey-bearded salts who declared, '. . . if it looks right, then it is right.' Far too many potentially good hulls have been spoilt by the addition of a monstrously misproportioned cabin, or a totally out-of-character bow or stern or by being stretched out of shape in order to accommodate more facilities than her size will permit – producing something more like a floating caravan.

If we compare the dimensions of two extreme boats we can gauge quite a useful picture of each. Our first example is described as having hardly any difference between her LOA and her LWL, she also has excessive beam and shallow draught. The difference between the LOA and LWL is known as the overhangs and the above example appears to have virtually no overhangs; it would also be a fair assumption to say she has a high freeboard. She is in fact a tub. She will be sluggish as she tries to push her bulky hull through the water and her freeboard will send her waddling sideways whenever the wind blows. She is probably quite old but she will have ample accommodation down below.

Right: The Dragon Class sloop is a fine example of a very fast hull shape with a narrow beam and long overhangs

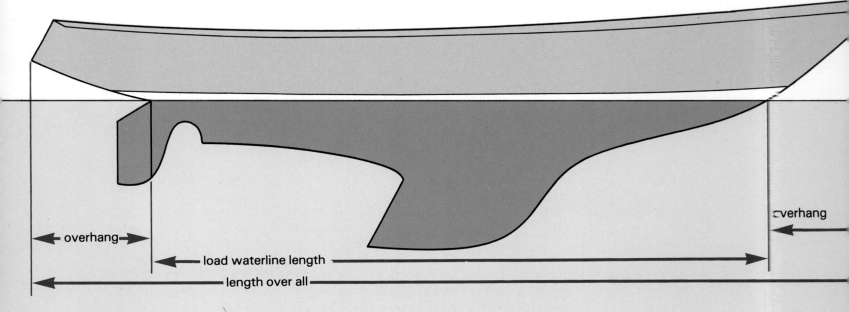

overhang

load waterline length

length over all

overhang

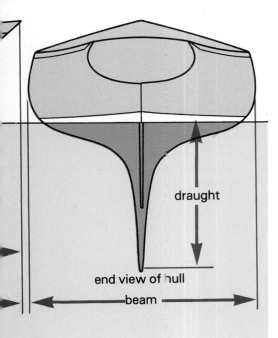

draught

end view of hull

beam

Our second example is vastly different. Described as having excessively long overhangs with a narrow beam and a deep draught, she will be fast. She will also be very wet as her needle-sharp bow cuts through the water with no ability to ride over the waves. A lot of water will come aboard and some of it is bound to find its way down your neck. If you tuck your elbows in you may get below but it is unlikely that you will be able to squeeze anything other than a wedge of cheese into her fine bow. Once again she is probably very old.

These are extreme examples of hull shape, but somewhere between the two you will find the ideal craft to suit your needs. Look for a boat with moderate overhangs and a clean entry of her bow into the water. A good modern boat will have a beam dimension which permits stability under sail and at the same time provides adequate accommodation below. Try to avoid any boat that displays exaggerations of styling and those that have been stuffed full of extra berths suggesting luxury. The extras usually mean that there is no room for the necessities. Standing headroom is definitely an advantage but it should not be achieved at the expense of the overall look of the boat. The line of the deck from stem to stern, the sheerline, is one of the most critical factors influencing the appearance of a boat, as is the cut of her bow and stern. A smooth gently curving sheerline running back to a soft counter stern or a nicely shaped transom will make all the difference to a boat's attraction. She should, without question, look right!

This boat with her more traditional long keel enjoys firm support when dried out alongside between tides.

KEEL SHAPE

A boat's performance is governed strongly by the type of keel fitted. Of the two major types, one is usually quite short like a broad knife blade protruding out from the bottom of the boat; this type is called a skeg keel. The skeg is very responsive to any movement of the tiller and will give the boat a high degree of manoeuvrability – a useful factor to be considered when navigating in congested waters. A skeg can make a vessel 'tender', that is, she will lean over quite sharply in a gust of wind. This is due to the lack of resistance of the small keel area to the water pressing against it. It is not unsafe for a boat to behave in this manner and once her maximum angle of heel has been reached she will sail quite comfortably. A skeg configuration also means that she will be a relatively fast boat.

A skeg's main disadvantages are its inability to take the ground safely (provide adequate safe support for the vessel when dried out) because of its small foot, and its unreliability when running before the wind. This latter drawback requires a very attentive helmsman on the tiller as the boat will constantly try to shoot off in all directions requiring frequent steering corrections to maintain the course.

The other main keel type, the long keel, is more traditional. Being long and straight it gives the boat much more directional stability. When running before the wind this consequently makes the helmsman's job far less exacting and strenuous. Manoeuvrability is less immediate than with a skeg but the tiller response is not sluggish. A long keel also provides a strong steady platform when taking the ground. If drying out alongside a harbour wall or jetty it will usually keep the boat in a fairly horizontal position, a reassuring fact to a crew that may be obliged to remain aboard. Because of the heavier construction used for a long keel, the boat will be slightly slower than a similarly sized vessel fitted with a skeg. As with most aspects of marine design, there are many varieties of keel shape but if the characteristics of these two basic types are remembered then you will be less likely to find yourself with a badly designed boat.

Some boats are fitted with two and even three keels, which allow their owners to use them in tidal areas which dry out completely. As the tide recedes they will sit comfortably on the mud supported by their two 'legs' until the water returns to float them off again.

Variations of keel
shape are numerous
but the five most
common are
(a) the fin and skeg,
(b) the long keel,
(c) bilge keels —
either two or three,
(d) the lifting keel,
and (e) the centre
plate.

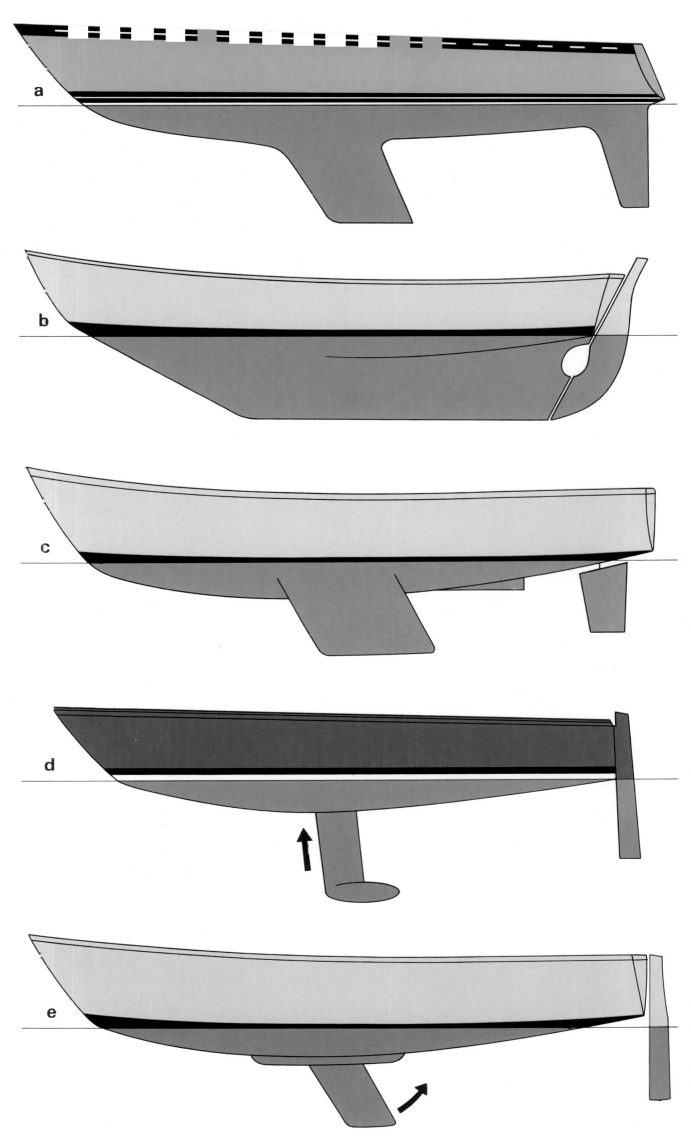

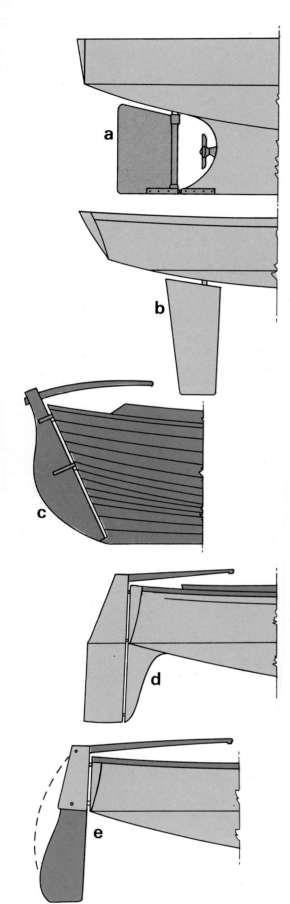

Yet another category is the retractable keel which allows a vessel to vary her draught according to the prevailing conditions. It has many advantages; it can be fully retracted to alleviate drag when sailing on a run, or fully extended to improve windward performance. When sailing in shallow waters where the exact depth is unknown, it can be lowered halfway and thus act as an early-warning system; as it scrapes the sea bed it can be retracted and the boat sailed off into deeper water.

STEERING

The rudder controls the direction of a vessel through the water and is activated by either a tiller or a wheel. The rudder is only effective if the boat has 'steerage way', that is, if she is moving faster than the water she is moving through. If a tiller is pushed over to the left (port) the boat will turn towards the right (starboard). If it is pushed over to the right the boat will turn to the left. Thus with a tiller the directional thrust will result in an opposite course. With a wheel steering arrangement, however, the direction taken corresponds to the direction of the thrust exerted. Turn the wheel to the right and the boat will turn to the right, and vice versa – just like driving a car.

Steering with a tiller is responsive and positive but it can sometimes be wet work as the helmsman has to remain at his post whatever the weather conditions. Wheel steering activates the movement of the rudder through a series of wire control lines and pulleys. If the system employed has been well fitted and the lines correctly adjusted for tension, then it is just as positive as tiller steering. It also retains one great advantage over the tiller: because of its control system it can be mounted within the confines of a snug enclosed cabin – well out of the weather.

When a rudder is mounted externally down the centre line of the stern it is said to be *transom hung*, and many boats are fitted with this arrangement. An alternative is to have the rudder mounted beneath the boat with its stock entering the hull below the waterline and passing up through a watertight tube to the steering position.

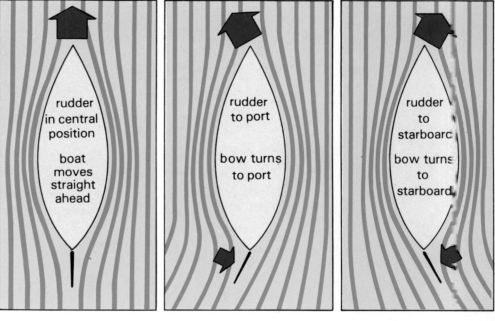

Above: The effect of rudder action on water flow around the hull.

Right: The movement of the tiller activates the rudder and so controls the direction taken by the boat.

Above: Examples of typical rudder types: (a) the motor-sailer type, (b) the balanced rudder, (c) the transom-hung 'Folkboat' type, (d) transom-hung with a skeg, and (e) the lifting type most commonly found on dinghies.

Opposite: A twin-keeled boat sits comfortably upright between tides. Note how her skeg rudder acts as a third leg.

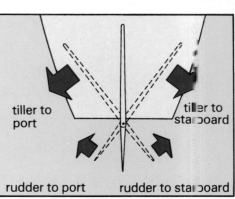

The cruiser-racer *Garuda II* beating into a stiff breeze. Under strong wind conditions a boat's rigging is subjected to very heavy loads and many of the larger boats are rigged with solid steel rod rigging.

RIGGING

On a sailing boat the rigging will fall into two distinct categories: the *standing rigging*, the wire stays and shrouds which support the mast, and the *running rigging*, which are the numerous lines used to control the sails. The lines used for hoisting up the sails are called halyards and they can be made of flexible steel wire, laid (twisted) rope or a combination of both. The lines for controlling the sails are called sheets and these are always made of braided rope.

The mast is supported in a fore-and-aft direction by two wire stays: the forestay leads from the masthead to the stem, and the backstay leads from the masthead to the centre of the stern. The mast is supported transversely by a pair of wires called cap shrouds, one to port and one to starboard. These lead from the masthead to the outer edge of the deck alongside the mast. If the cap shrouds were led down in a direct line the angle between them and the mast would be too acute for safety, so they are braced out from the mast on each end of a small spar set about a third of the way down the mast. These spars, called crosstrees, increase the angle made between mast and shroud and supply greater stability. It is only on quite small vessels with shortish masts that it is possible to dispense with the need for crosstrees.

The lower part of the mast is further stiffened by the addition of matched pairs of wires, called lower shrouds, leading from just below the crosstrees and ending at the outer edge of the deck. The number of lower shrouds fitted is somewhat dependent on the size of boat but the average small sloop will have two lower shrouds per side.

All these shrouds and stays are secured to the hull by strong steel fixings, called chainplates, built into the structure of the hull. Adjustments to tension at the lower ends of the stays are made by bottlescrews which can be loosened or tightened until the mast is correctly stepped and straight.

The halyards can be either flexible steel wire or rope, and are used for hoisting the sails into position. The mainsail halyard travels from the foot of the mast to the masthead and passes through a sheave (the wheel part of a block) to exit aft; it then falls back down the length of the mast to the level of the boom where it can be connected to the head of the mainsail. The foresail halyard also travels up the mast but exits forward. Many modern boats have the halyards rigged inside the mast itself, which reduces both wind resistance and noise. The halyards can either be cleated off (secured) at the foot of the mast or led back through suitably placed fairleads to the cockpit and secured there.

To control the mainsail once it is hoisted, there is a mainsheet attached to the end of the boom. This is made up as a purchase (device to improve pulling power) through a series of blocks and is secured firmly in the cockpit. When the mainsail is down, the boom is supported by a halyard called a topping lift.

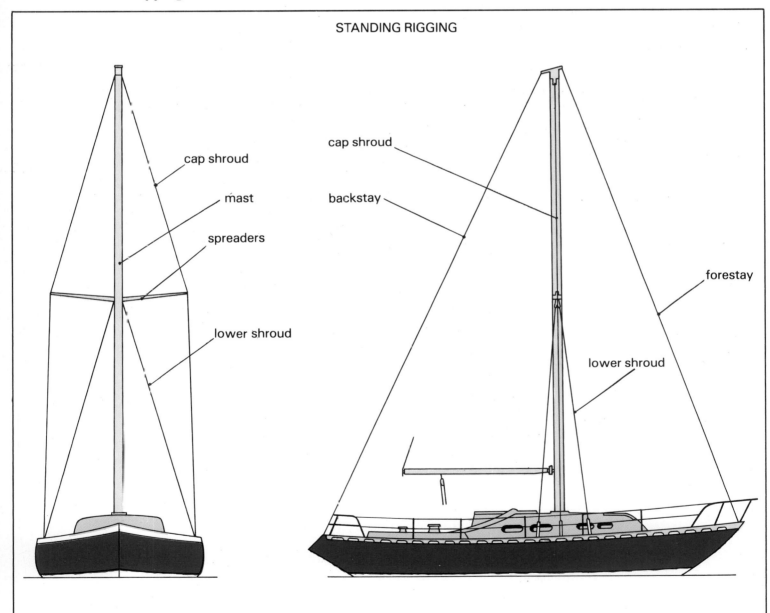

STANDING RIGGING

cap shroud

mast

spreaders

lower shroud

cap shroud

backstay

forestay

lower shroud

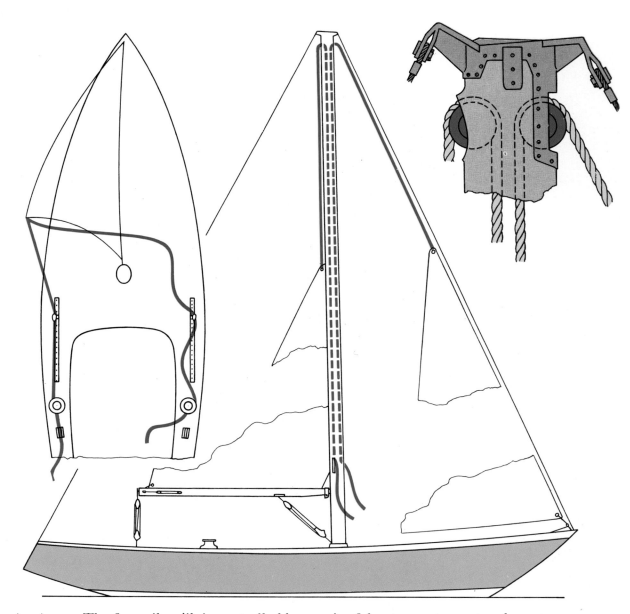

The basic running rig on a typical Bermudan sloop. The jib sheets are seen from above on the left while the elevation shows the two main halyards. These are rigged internally through the mast and the detail shows the masthead arrangement of the two halyard sheaves.

The foresail or jib is controlled by a pair of sheets, one to port and one to starboard, which are both attached to the rear corner of the sail and led back from there to the cockpit. They travel first through a block mounted on the side deck and then on to a winch before being cleated off. The jib sheet block is frequently mounted on a sliding track which gives fore-and-aft adjustment depending on the size of headsail being used. The additional power provided by a winch greatly assists the crewman in achieving the correct tension for trimming the foresail: only on very small craft is a winch unnecessary.

SAILS

On a typical sloop there are two sails, a mainsail and a jib, and as we are using a Bermudan sloop for our example, they will both be triangular. The combined size and cut of these sails forms the boat's sail plan which has been designed to give the boat good sailing balance. A badly balanced boat is not only difficult to handle but can also be dangerous.

Correct sail balance is very important. Ideally, when the tiller is released with both sails hoisted, the boat should ease her head up into the wind where she will stop in her tracks with the sails idly flapping. If she has a tendency to drift off the wind, then she could well be blown over on to her side and founder. The former condition is called *weather helm* and the latter is called *lee helm*. The jib should be large enough to allow control without being in any way overpowering. If its size is excessive compared to the area of the mainsail, it will blow the boat's bow away from the wind with a similar result.

The names of the parts of a sail remain the same whether applied to a jib or a mainsail. The top corner is the head, the bottom forward corner is the tack and the rear lower corner is the clew. The three sides are also named: working clockwise from the front edge, they are the *luff*, the *foot* and the

Right: The mainsail luff sliders in the mast track.

Below: Hanking on the luff clips of the foresail to the forestay.

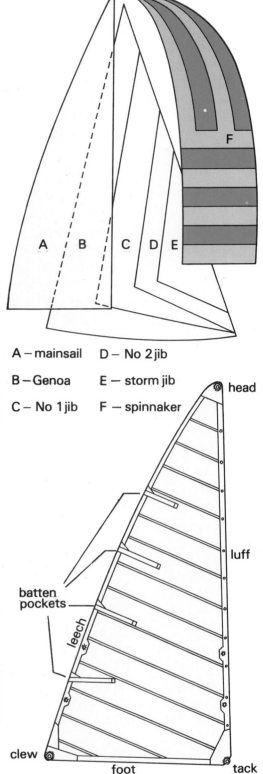

A – mainsail	D – No 2 jib
B – Genoa	E – storm jib
C – No 1 jib	F – spinnaker

Top: A typical sail plan for a Bermudan sloop.

Above: The parts of a mainsail. These names are applicable to both the mainsail and the foresail.

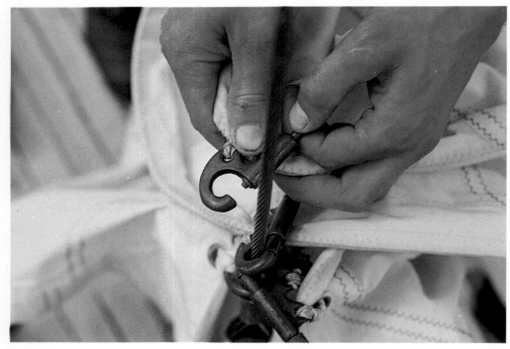

leech. The mainsail is usually fitted with long pockets sewn at intervals along the leech for the insertion of wooden or plastic battens. The purpose of these is to stiffen the leech which improves the airflow and makes the sail more efficient.

The mainsail is hoisted up with its luff fed into a slot in the mast which starts just above the boom and travels to the masthead. Its foot is located in a similar slot in the top of the boom. The clew of the mainsail is tightened with an outhaul purchase fitted at the end of the boom. The jib is fitted with a series of clips along the length of its luff, and these are attached to the forestay on which the sail is hoisted. The jib's tack is secured to the stemhead and the clew to the jib sheets.

To get the maximum efficiency from the sails it is essential that the luff of each is tightened up stiffly. Both the halyards may well pass around a winch on the sides of the mast, one for the jib and one for the main, which enable a good tension to be achieved. If no winches are fitted then alternative methods can be used. The boom can be fitted with a downhaul which will pull it down thus tightening the luff of the main; or the tack of the jib can be attached to an outhaul purchase at the stem and led back down the foredeck where it can be cleated off.

The Principles of Sailing

It is not difficult to understand how a large area of sail presented square-on to the wind will be blown along and thus move the hull platform supporting it. This is the principle which drove the square-rigged ships around the world. The effectiveness of the fore-and-aft rig is based on an entirely different principle, and while this will allow a boat to sail into the wind it will only be able to do so at an angle.

The term *close to the wind* is the expression relating to this angle and it is generally accepted to be about 45 degrees at its finest. In other words, with a wind blowing from due north a boat will only be able to make a course either to the north-west or the north-east. If the vessel is pointed up close to the wind, thus reducing the angle below 45 degrees, its efficiency will rapidly decrease.

As the wind reaches the sail it splits into two separate airflows, one passing on either side of the sail from the luff to the leech. The airflow to windward (the direction the wind is coming from) passes round the inner curve of the sail with virtually no change in speed. The airflow on the leeward side, however, has further to travel and therefore its speed increases. This increase in speed causes a reduction in pressure which in turn creates a vacuum on the leeward side of the sail. It is this vacuum that sucks the sail forward. This then is the basic principle, albeit simplified, of the fore-and-aft driving force.

With a conventional sloop rig this principle operates for both the foresail and the mainsail, each one contributing its own driving force. However, with the two sails rigged closely together a second factor comes into action.

A mixed selection of dinghy types enjoy a crisp afternoon's racing.

A helmsman's view of his sails — well trimmed for beating.

The airflow from the windward side of the jib accelerates the airflow on the leeward side of the mainsail and forces it through the slot between the two sails. This slot effect is known as the *venturi principle* and it results in the combination of the two sails producing a power output greater than the sum of their individual efforts.

SAIL TRIMMING

Trimming the sails correctly is critical if top performance is to be achieved. We have already mentioned the need for the luff of both the sails to be taut. A taut luff will present a clean leading edge to the wind, creating a smooth airflow with a minimum of turbulence.

With the mainsail gently flapping, start to tighten it by hauling in on the mainsheet. The leech of the sail will begin to smooth itself out first but there may still remain some fluttering at the luff. Continue to harden in (haul in)

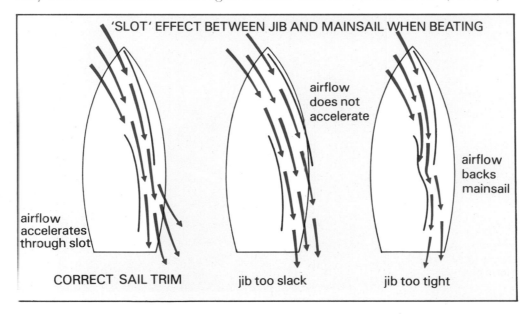

'SLOT' EFFECT BETWEEN JIB AND MAINSAIL WHEN BEATING

airflow does not accelerate

airflow accelerates through slot

airflow backs mainsail

CORRECT SAIL TRIM

jib too slack

jib too tight

the sail until just after this fluttering stops. At this point the sail will be working at its best performance.

Next the foresail is sheeted in and the luff turbulence ironed out in the same way. As this is done keep an eye on the mainsail. If the jib is over tightened it will narrow the slot between the sails too much and impair its efficiency. The jib will then 'back' the main, creating turbulence on its leeward side and making the luff bubble out to windward. If this occurs, ease the jib sheet until a smooth airflow is achieved on both sails.

It is very tempting for the novice sailor to over-tighten the sails, but with all the sheets as hard as iron bars he is getting far from the best out of the boat. In fact all that he has done is create a stiff obstruction for the wind to flatten. The boat will heel over excessively, thus presenting a much shorter mast and leading edge of sail to the wind. The further the boat heels the less effective it becomes. Ease all the sheets and allow the boat to straighten up and sail more effectively. By decreasing the angle of heel the sails become more efficient and more power will be extracted from the wind. Too great an angle of heel will also mean that the keel will offer less resistance to the water pressure acting on it and the boat will travel sideways faster than she moves forwards. This sideways movement is known as *leeway*, and despite the ship's apparent direction it can make a drastic difference to the actual course the vessel finally achieves. Leeway is never absent when a sailing boat is under way but efforts should always be made to keep it to a minimum.

POINTS OF SAILING

When a boat sails close to the wind she is said to be *beating*. Close-hauled, with the sheets hard in (this is an instance where they should be hauled in tight) is taxing for the helmsman. He must pay constant attention to the sails to get the best performance out of the vessel and make the most headway against an opposing wind. If he attempts to point the boat too close up into the wind, known as *pinching*, then the luffs will start to flutter and the boat will slow down. At the same time her leeway will rapidly increase as she is blown sideways. Conversely, if the helmsman sails too far off the wind the vessel will heel excessively, again increase her leeward drift and, in strong

The diagram shows the point of sailing known as 'beating', the centre boat is in 'irons'.

Although possessing an exceptionally clean bottom this is a classic example of excessive heeling and the boat's performance will rapidly deteriorate.

Racing on a broad reach with all spinnakers set can provide excellent sailing.

winds, there is a danger that she will broach (lie flat on her side at right-angles to the wind). The boat's head should be eased off the wind just enough to avoid the luff of each sail from fluttering.

Reaching is the fastest point of sailing. If the wind comes from anywhere between 45 degrees off the bow and abeam (from the side, at 90 degrees) it is known as a close reach, and on this point of sailing the sails will generate their maximum power output. If the wind continues round until it is between the beam and 45 degrees off the stern quarter it is said to be a broad reach. Broad reaching can be the perfect point for relaxed and efficient sailing.

Running before the wind, with the wind directly behind the stern, requires close attention to the sails and a sensitive hand on the tiller. The mainsheet is loosened off to allow the boom to swing out, presenting the maximum area of sail to the wind. The boat is being pushed along and the large mainsail will blanket off the smaller area of the jib which will flap away idly in front of it. To make use of the jib it can be taken over to windward, on the opposite side to the boomed-out mainsail. The jib may well need its own boom (whisker pole) to keep it well out; a boathook, or spare spinnaker boom can also be used for this purpose. You have now 'square-rigged' your sloop and this method of trimming the sails for a run is known as *goose-winging*.

When running, care should be taken to keep the wind within the mainsail. If your attention wanders and the wind moves round behind the sail it could cause the boom to crash over from one side of the boat to the other – to *gybe*. A sudden unintentional occurrence such as this is not only disturbing but can also cause serious damage to both boat and crew.

It is important to maintain a correct balance between the sails on a run. If the mainsail is too large for the size of jib being used it will cause the vessel to yaw (swing) wildly about, and if the wind should increase in strength it will very soon make the boat uncontrollable. The excessive mainsail area will lift the stern of the boat which will then try to overtake the bows. In mild weather, when the mainsail tries to take command a larger headsail should be rigged to balance it, but if this is the result of an increase in wind strength then the mainsail should be reefed down (decreased in size, see Chapter 3) or lowered altogether and the passage continued under headsails alone.

Top and above: Diagrams showing the points of sailing for reaching and running respectively.

TACKING, GOING ABOUT AND GYBING

It is time to look at the manoeuvres required to alter a vessel's direction. Let us examine, for example, a boat making passage along a wide estuary with the wind against her. The boat starts off beating into the wind on the port tack, that is, with the wind on her port-hand side. Eventually she will find herself close to the starboard bank of the estuary where she will need to alter direction to avoid running aground. The skipper will have to put the boat about and change on to the starboard tack.

The helmsman alerts his crew of his intention with the cry 'Ready about!' The crewman stands by at the jib-sheets ready to make the necessary adjustments. When the helmsman judges it safe, and when the sails are drawing well, he gives his second command 'Lee-oh!' and puts the tiller over to leeward, which turns the boat up into the eye of the wind. The wind passes round to the starboard side of the boat's head and fills the sails from the other side. The mainsail boom swings over to port and simultaneously the crewman releases the starboard jib-sheet and lets the jib also travel round to the port side of the mast. The helmsman continues his turn on to the other tack, and as the mainsail starts to draw and the boat gathers way the crewman hardens in the port jib-sheet and trims the sail. The vessel now continues up the estuary on the starboard tack.

This operation is called *going about* and it should be executed smoothly and positively. If the helmsman displays any hesitation or uncertainty or if the vessel is not carrying enough way (speed) then it can end up pointing straight into the eye of the wind. She will completely lose all forward motion and will just sit there with her sails flapping idly. When this occurs she is said to be *in irons*, and all the embarrassed helmsman can do is bear away, pick up more speed and try the manoeuvre again. Being in irons is not in itself dangerous except maybe to other vessels in the vicinity who expected the boat to go about, but it does waste both time and sea-room (space to manoeuvre).

When faced with a fluky wind or a particularly lumpy sea, there is a variation on going about which can prove more successful. The same initial steps are taken, but as the boat's head comes through the eye of the wind the crewman holds on to the starboard jib-sheet for a second or two longer than in the previous instance. The jib will then 'back' and this will help by blowing the bows of the boat round on to the new tack. Once her head is clearly round, the sheet is released and the foresail hardened in as before.

It is clear that our sloop will need to make several alterations in her course to navigate up the estuary against the wind. She will be obliged to zig-zag,

The diagram shows the changes of tack and the various points of sailing required for the boat to round the headland.

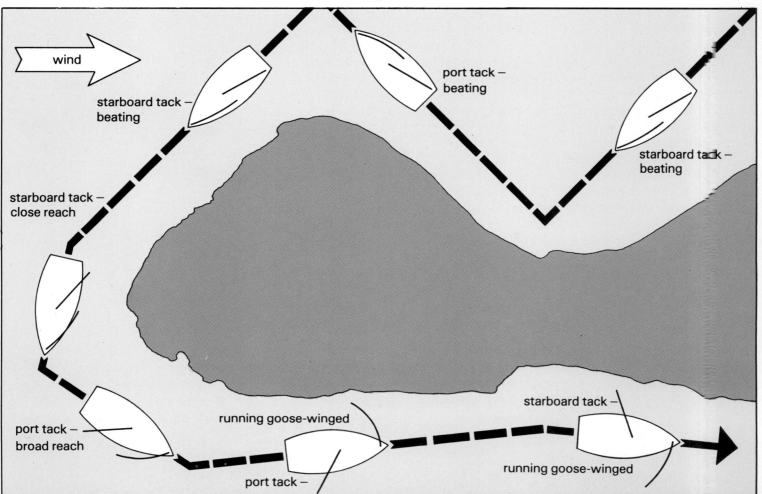

wind

starboard tack –
beating

port tack –
beating

starboard tack –
beating

starboard tack –
close reach

port tack –
broad reach

running goose-winged

port tack –

starboard tack –

running goose-winged

or *tack*, an inevitable procedure when making ground against the prevailing wind.

When a similar change of course is necessary but when the wind is from behind the manoeuvre is called *gybing* and it should be carried out with some caution. On this point of sailing the mainsail will be under the greatest pressure, so this is the sail to concentrate on. The jib can be eased and left to flap behind the mainsail. The tiller is then gently brought over to guide the vessel's stern into the eye of the wind. This should always be done smoothly and without any heavy-handed movements.

Simultaneously the slack in the mainsheet should be taken in and the boom hauled inboard towards the centre of the boat. As the wind passes across the stern the boom will swing over, but it now has a shorter distance to travel. The mainsheet should immediately be eased, allowing the boom to swing right out and put the boat on its new tack. The jib can now be sheeted in by the crewman and its trim adjusted accordingly.

Tacking during close racing requires skilful helmsmanship and careful judgment if a collision is to be avoided.

Seamanship

In the Introduction the need for forethought was mentioned and nowhere is this more important than in the practice of seamanship. At sea, miles from land, a minor error of judgment can be passed over, but if the same error is made within the confines of a busy harbour the consequences can be dangerous and expensive. The rule should always be to think through your intentions in advance, to execute them slowly and surely and to have an alternative plan ready in case things do not turn out as anticipated. This is especially relevant when preparing to moor a boat.

Tying up alongside is probably the most common form of mooring. It may be against a harbour wall, a jetty, a marina pontoon or even alongside another boat. The procedure is the same in all cases. It would be unwise for a novice to enter a busy harbour and approach a mooring under sail alone, so I will deal with these procedures with the boat under power and the sails lowered.

In most harbours and marinas the authorities will direct a visiting craft to a vacant berth. When this occurs do not go straight into the space indicated – circle around and examine the berth from a safe distance. There may be an unseen obstacle such as a small dinghy, which you will only spot if you make a preliminary tour.

Once you have decided that the berth is suitable, make ready the warps (mooring ropes) and fenders you are likely to need. If there is a tide running the boat should always make its approach from down-tide, and this will determine which side to rig the warps and fenders (either to port or

The boat in the foreground is moored to a single swinging mooring whereas those in the background are moored to twin buoys – fore-and-aft.

These fenders are sensibly positioned: they are not squeezed tightly against the jetty and allow movement of the boat with no danger of the fenders being pushed out of place.

starboard). Initially you will only need a bow line and a stern line, each made fast to a suitable cleat on the deck. If the vessel is fitted with guard rails, the warps should be led through the rails from the cleat and brought back inboard over the top of the rail and coiled neatly on the deck. They will then be ready to hand and will not distort the rails when put under tension. No seaman likes to cruise around with fenders dangling along his topsides; they can be tied in place and left on the side decks ready to be kicked overboard as the boat draws alongside the mooring. If you are uncertain which way the tide is running, look at the other boats to see which way they are lying – which of their lines, bow or stern, is slack and which way their dinghies are swinging.

The final approach should be made slowly and carefully. A crew member moves to the foredeck to handle the bow line, kicking the fenders over as he goes; the helmsman controls the stern line. The vessel's headway should be reduced to a minimum so that she stops gently alongside and about a foot away from the mooring. The speed of the boat should be just enough to match that of the tide; too fast an approach will require a gear change into reverse and a touch on the throttle to slow her down, but if this can be avoided it is far more seamanlike.

If there is someone ashore to take the lines, the job of tying up is relatively simple. If, however, there is no one around, then the bow hand will need to step ashore as the boat draws near and make fast the line. He should remember that he is not hauling in the *Queen Mary* and should not pull excessively on the bow line. If he does, the boat's rounded shape will pivot the stern far out away from the mooring, thus rendering the helmsman helpless. The bow hand should exert just enough tension to hold the bows before he secures the line. He can then walk back towards the stern and take the stern line from the helmsman to make that fast. With both lines secure the engine can be switched off.

Further lines can now be rigged: breast ropes, one from the bow and one from the stern, are led directly across to the shore and 'springs' are added to stop the boat surging to and fro. The springs are led diagonally from the bow and stern to suitable cleats or fixings on the mooring.

All these lines should be tensioned to allow enough space for the fenders to operate successfully. If they are too tight the fenders will be crushed or, worse still, they could be forced out of place and the boat damaged.

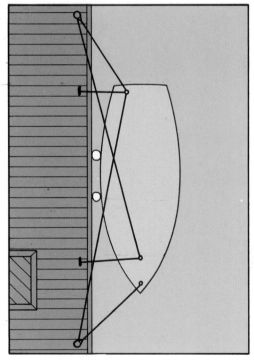

Mooring alongside with two breast ropes, two diagonally rigged springs and a line at bow and stern.

To moor between piles, on 'trots', you need only a bow and stern line. Once again the mooring should be approached from down-tide. Nose the bows slowly up to the post and slip the bow line through the ring attached to the chain on the post slider. The bow line can then be paid out so that the stern slips back to the second post where the stern line can be made fast. Finally, centre up the vessel between the two posts and cut the engine. If the boat fails to fall back directly towards the rear post and the stern swings out away from it, you will have to launch the tender to take out the stern line. Provided you have approached the first post from down-tide there will be no danger in this and your vessel will not swing right round and damage other moored boats.

A swinging mooring is simply a buoy secured to the sea-bed with either a pair of anchors or a heavy concrete block. On the top of the buoy is a ring or 'pick-up' line. As the vessel draws up to the buoy, the bow hand can catch the ring or line with a boathook and attach his line. Swinging moorings are sometimes rigged with a light line that is attached to the main mooring line a few feet below the water. If so, haul in the buoy and the light line until the heavier line is reached. The bow line should always be attached to the heavy mooring line.

ANCHORING A VESSEL

Whereas a boat can be left safely on any of the above moorings it is unwise, unless absolutely necessary and in favourable weather conditions, to leave a boat unattended on her anchor. There will be occasions when it is necessary to anchor to wait out a foul (opposing) tide or to shelter from bad weather behind a headland – or even just for a bite of lunch and a swim. Whatever the reason the things to watch for are the state of the tide, whether it is high or low water or somewhere between the two, the depth of water available under the vessel and the state of the sea-bed – whether it is mud, sand, shale, weed or rocks. The main bow anchor should be stowed on the foredeck and any lashings should be easy to release.

The boat should be headed up into the tide and brought to a stop, then as she begins to make sternway (fall backwards) the anchor should be lowered, not thrown, overboard. Enough cable should be paid out to equal at least three times the depth of water under the boat's keel. If the tide is still rising then more cable will have to be veered out as the depth of water increases.

Most modern boats are supplied with an anchor rope (warp) but unless it is a small craft the anchor will be more effective if it is attached to a chain. The additional weight of the chain makes it lie along the sea-bed which considerably improves the holding power of the anchor. If a rope warp is used then a couple of fathoms of chain (1 fathom = 6 feet/1·8 metres) should be shackled to the end of the warp and then to the anchor; this will help to

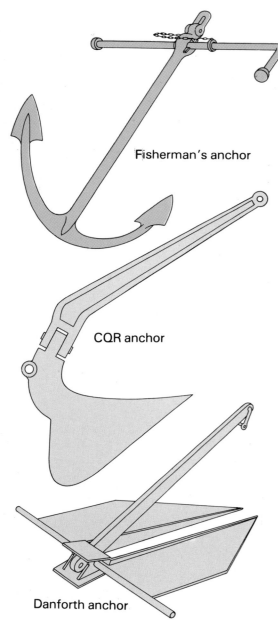

Fisherman's anchor

CQR anchor

Danforth anchor

Above: The three most common types of anchor.
Right: The diagram shows the minimum scope of cable required for safe anchoring.

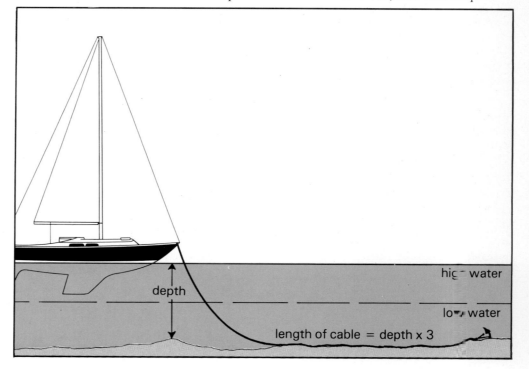

depth

high water

low water

length of cable = depth x 3

A neat foredeck stowage for a CQR anchor. The lashings make it quickly accessible for use.

achieve the same result. Where chain is used throughout then the inboard end should never be secured with a shackle, it should always be lashed. In an emergency the lashing can be cut through, whereas a jammed shackle could prove disastrous.

An anchor can sometimes be difficult to break free, and as a precaution a trip line can be attached to the anchor before it is lowered. The trip line is attached to the head of the anchor and if the latter becomes fouled (caught on an underwater obstruction), the trip line is hauled up and the anchor broken free. If you are anchoring close to other vessels, remember that as the tide falls your scope of chain will increase so always allow yourself plenty of room for error. The turn of the tide will also cause the anchor to trip and rebury itself and this can also mean a drag of quite a few feet.

As well as the main anchor it is advisable to carry a second anchor, a spare or *kedge*, and this can either be stowed on the foredeck alongside the bow anchor or kept in a cockpit locker. It should be rigged with a nylon warp.

This diagram shows an anchor rigged with a trip line. Should the anchor fail to break free the line is recovered by lifting the floating buoy and then hauling it in to release the anchor. The trip line is always attached to the head of the anchor.

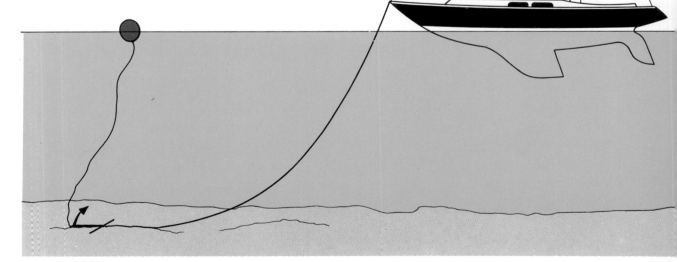

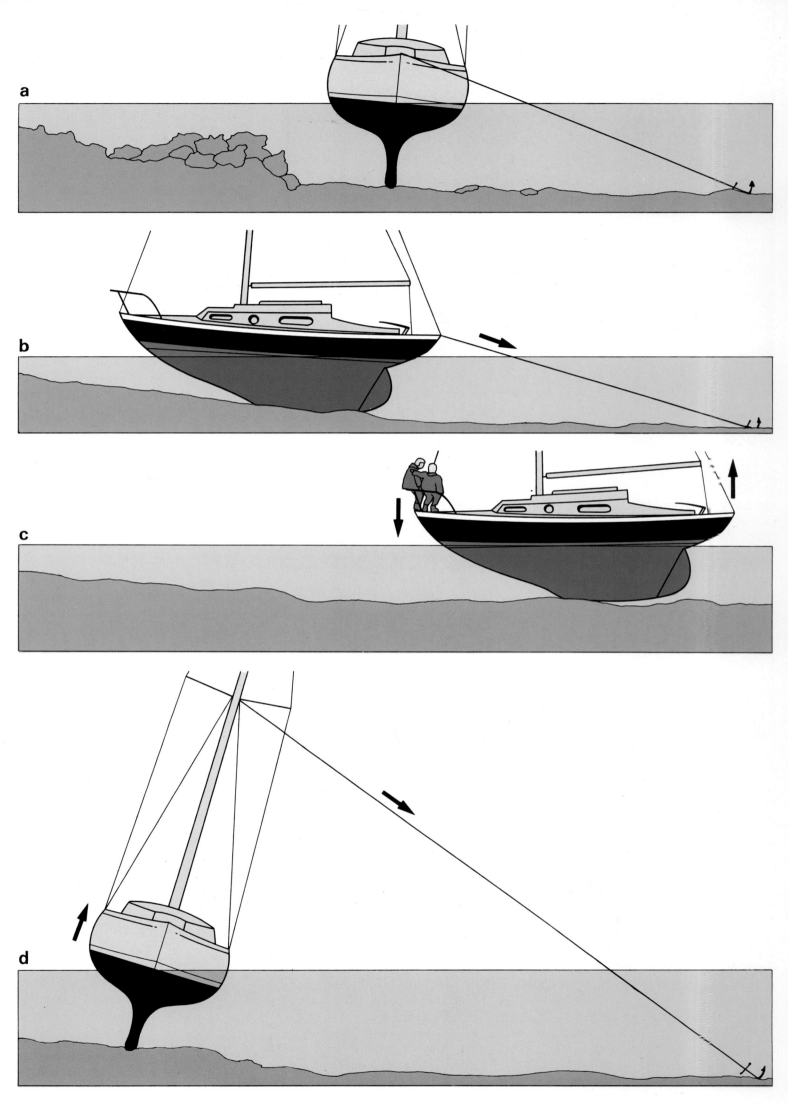

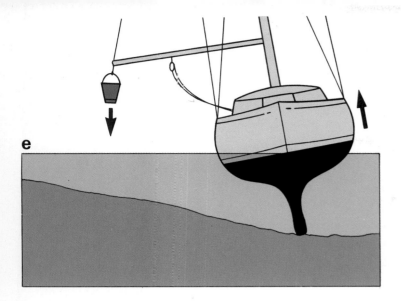
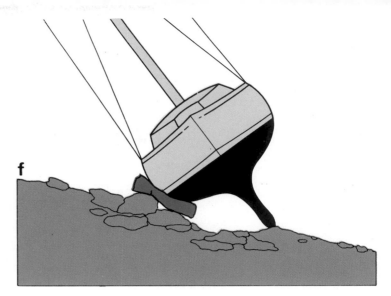

RUNNING AGROUND

An experienced sailor will never willingly admit to making this error of judgment. Do not be deceived – the seaman has yet to be met who hasn't at some time or other sailed his boat too close to a sandbank only to stay there admiring the view for several hours. In fair weather this is usually the only penalty to pay, plus a deal of embarrassment, but if the weather conditions are bad then every effort should be made to refloat the vessel before any damage is sustained. With anything other than a fin keel a boat will sit fairly upright, but most fin-keelers will lay well over at a sharp angle. So the following section is based on what happens to a fin-keeled boat.

If a vessel runs aground on a flood (rising) tide then there are three things to do. The first is to drop the sails to prevent the wind driving the boat further on to the bank. The second is to take the kedge anchor well out into deeper water, haul in the warp until the anchor bites and make it fast to the bows. The third and final thing is to wait. When the boat does begin to float give a pull on the kedge anchor and move her into deeper water. The sails can now be reset, the kedge retrieved and the boat can continue on her way.

Getting off on a falling tide is, however, a totally different matter. Time is the most critical factor, and all attempts to refloat the vessel should be made as quickly as possible. Don't immediately drop the sails – it takes too much time. Instead, gybe the boat and this may be just enough for her to free herself and sail off the bank on the other tack.

If this fails, free all the sheets and despatch the entire crew up to the foredeck. Their added weight in the bows will upset the vessel's trim, and as most fin keels are slightly shallower at the bow than at the stern she may well float. If she does, then a quick burst on the engine in reverse will back her off into safer waters. If this also fails, the kedge anchor should be laid out in line astern. Then, with the aid of the engine, you can try to pull her off.

Sometimes if the bank you are sitting on has a fairly shallow contour, the boat can be rocked off – heeling her one way and then the other can often loosen the grip on her keel and set her free. A heavy weight, such as an anchor, can be swung out on the end of the boom to create an exaggerated heel and this can also float her free.

If all these remedies fail, then the long wait is on and precautions should be taken to protect the hull from damage. On a sloping bank, and while some water still remains, the vessel should be heeled over to face away from the next incoming tide. If she is facing into the tide she may well fill with water before she refloats, particularly if the weather turns nasty. Once again, lay out the kedge into deep water to stop her being driven further on to the bank. If the ground is soft mud or sand the hull will not be harmed, but if the boat has grounded on stones then steps should be taken to safeguard the hull. Berth mattresses or cushions or even a spare sail should be lowered over the side between the hull and the ground and lashed in place. Where there are large rocks it is more advisable to jam a plank or the dinghy oars beneath the hull, but these should be well padded. Finally, don't forget to check the ship's battery – it may have been dislodged causing an acid leak into the boat.

Never panic if you run aground. If the situation appears exceptionally dangerous a distress flare should be fired. Think very carefully before taking this step, but it is not one to be ashamed of if the circumstances merit it.

Opposite and above: Methods of getting afloat after running aground: (a) an anchor taken out abeam. If hauling fails to refloat the vessel at least the anchor will stop her driving on to the rocks, (b) a line run out astern, (c) the crew weight moved as far forward as possible, (d) with an anchor out abeam the line is hauled tight with a halyard thus heeling the boat and reducing her draft, (e) a weight swung out on the boom will sometimes have the same effect, and lastly, (f) what to do if all else fails – protect the side of the boat from damage with a berth mattress or something similar.

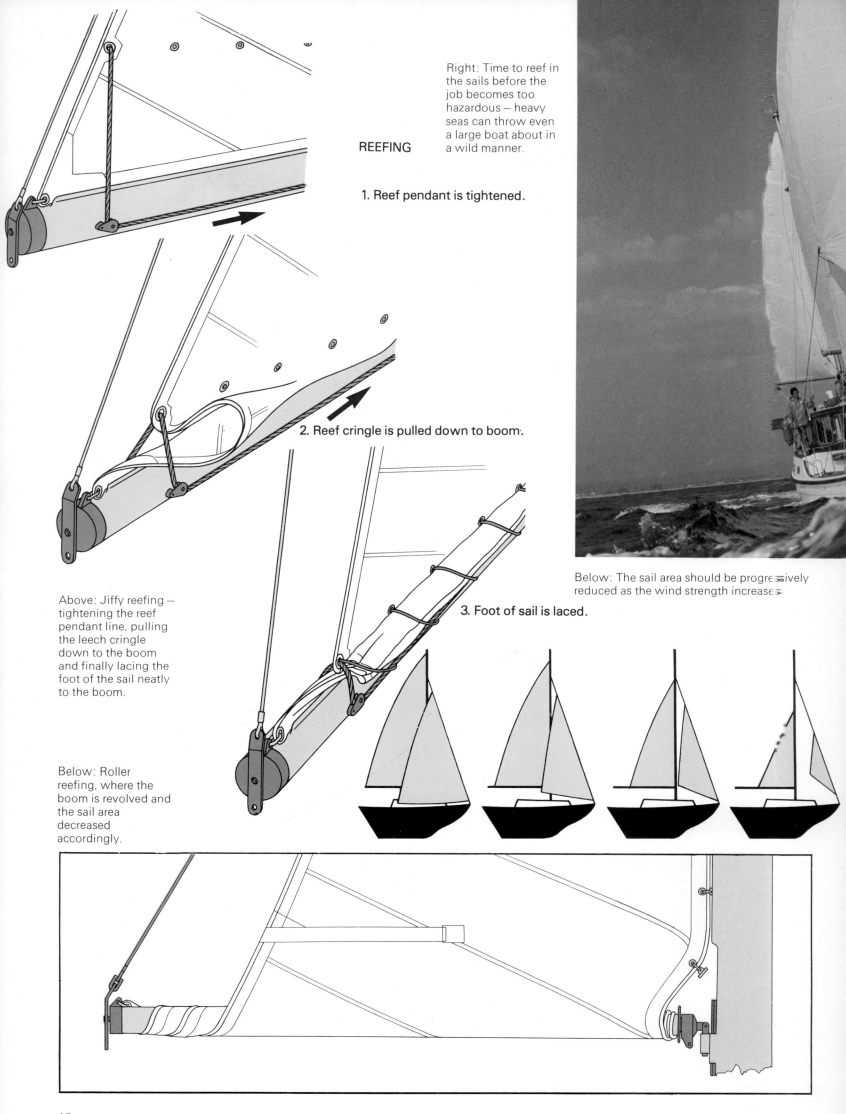

Right: Time to reef in the sails before the job becomes too hazardous — heavy seas can throw even a large boat about in a wild manner.

REEFING

1. Reef pendant is tightened.

2. Reef cringle is pulled down to boom.

3. Foot of sail is laced.

Above: Jiffy reefing — tightening the reef pendant line, pulling the leech cringle down to the boom and finally lacing the foot of the sail neatly to the boom.

Below: Roller reefing, where the boom is revolved and the sail area decreased accordingly.

Below: The sail area should be progressively reduced as the wind strength increases.

REEFING

When the weather conditions deteriorate and the wind strength increases, most sloops carrying full sail will soon find themselves hard pressed and it will be time to reduce the sail area, or reef down. With a small craft you should drop the headsail and set a smaller sail in its place. On larger vessels, the foresail is sometimes rigged with a built-in furling mechanism. Very simply it consists of a drum fitted to the foot of the forestay and controlled by a furling line led back to the cockpit. When this line is pulled the sail winds itself around the stay like a roller blind, thus reducing the area; release the furling line and haul on the jib sheet and the sail unwinds itself again.

The mainsail area can be reduced in two ways. The first is by the old-fashioned method of slab-reefing, where the lower part of the sail is simply folded and tied down to the top of the boom. The sail is made with a series of eyelets sewn into it, called *cringles*, which are placed at intervals up the leech of the sail. From the leech these eyelets cross the sail parallel to the boom to finish at the luff beside the mast. The luff and leech cringles are first made fast to the boom, the main halyard having been eased to let the sail drop down sufficiently; the weight of the boom is taken up by the topping lift. A light line is then threaded through the remaining eyes to 'lace' the sail snugly down to the boom. The modern version of slab-reefing is known as *jiffy reefing*, and with this system all the cringle down-hauls are pre-rigged along the length of the sail. At the pull of a line the sail is automatically wrapped up along the boom.

The second way to reef, and a common alternative to slab-reefing, is roller reefing. This method employs a geared mechanism fitted to the gooseneck (the attachment of the boom to the mast), which when operated by a handle revolves the boom. The main halyard is eased and the reefing handle turned, and as the boom revolves the sail is wound around it until the correct area of sail is achieved to suit the prevailing conditions.

The most important thing to remember about reefing is that it should be executed in good time. If a decision to reef is delayed until the last minute the weather may then be so bad as to make the operation slow and dangerous – if not impossible.

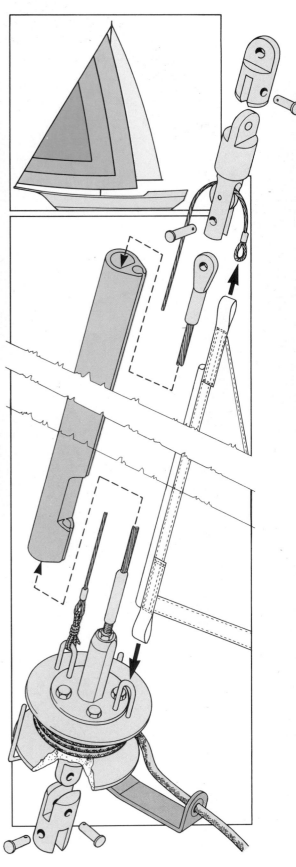

A jib furling mechanism. The inset shows how the sail can be reduced in area to suit the prevailing weather conditions.

Above: The complex
rigging of the *Cutty
Sark* forms an
intricate tracery
against the sky as she
sits in permanent
dock at Greenwich
on the River Thames.

Right: The correct
way to belay (tie off)
a halyard to a cleat.

Right: Coiling the tail
of a halyard and
making it secure to
the mast cleat.

Far right: Coiling and
securing a length of
rope.

ROPES AND ROPEWORK

The proper use of ropes is the mark of a good seaman and a basic knowledge of the various types available and their applications is an essential grounding for anyone who puts to sea under sail. The ropes found on modern craft are made from synthetic materials such as nylon, Terylene, polypropylene and polythene. Natural-fibre ropes of hemp, flax and cotton, with their inherent tendency to rot, are seldom used today.

As mentioned in Chapter 1, rope is either laid (twisted) or braided (plaited), and as the lay of a rope is usually right-handed it should be coiled in a left-handed or clockwise direction. Braided rope has no distinct lay so it can be coiled either way. Some braids, however, do seem to have their own particular bias and when this is the case only practice will reveal their preference.

Braided rope is very easy to handle and braided Terylene is therefore used for all sheets. Terylene is also suitable for halyards but care must be taken to use only the non-stretch type. With nylon rope, stretch can be an asset and it is suitable for use as a warp either for an anchor or for mooring. Its flexibility alleviates snubbing and it absorbs shock very well indeed. Polythene and polypropylene are cheaper ropes and their main advantage is their buoyancy – because of their ability to float they are ideal for use as 'pick-up' lines on moorings.

Tying off a rope-end securely is an integral part of any sailing activity. A novice may well admire his latest 'fist-like' knot but let him, or anyone else, try to undo it! A rope should be just as easy to release as it is to secure and the illustration clearly shows the correct way to secure a rope to a cleat.

A good seaman need not know how to tie a thousand knots but a few, well learnt, will prove invaluable. The following selection are those knots most commonly used on board a modern sailing vessel.

Figure-of-eight knot Used at the end of a rope to increase its diameter. It is the knot used at the tail end of a sheet to prevent it running out through the sheet block.

Bowline For making an eye or loop at the end of a rope; this is a particularly useful knot with many applications – it is easily undone whether wet or dry.

Reef knot Primarily used for joining together two ropes of equal thickness. It is sometimes difficult to undo when wet.

Sheet bend Used for attaching the jib sheets to the clew of a sail. It is also useful for joining together ropes of unequal thickness.

Fisherman's knot Used for joining together two lengths of very thin line. When wet it is virtually impossible to undo.

Round turn and two half hitches An excellent knot for securing a rope to a post or spar – for example, a mooring post. It will not slip and is easy to release either wet or dry.

Clove hitch A good knot that will not slip but one to be used with caution; it can be very difficult to release especially when one part is under tension.

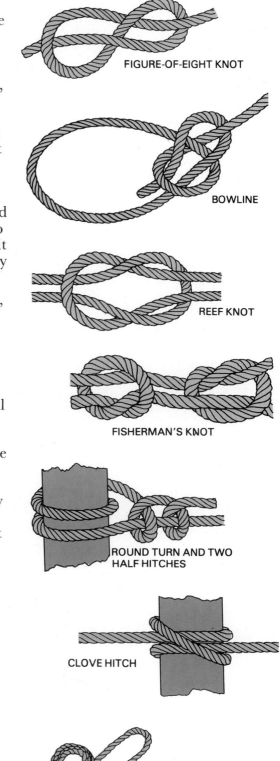

FIGURE-OF-EIGHT KNOT

BOWLINE

REEF KNOT

FISHERMAN'S KNOT

ROUND TURN AND TWO HALF HITCHES

CLOVE HITCH

Above: One major advantage of an inflatable dinghy is that even when stopping only for a short stay it will do no harm to the sides of the boat when tethered alongside.

Below: When a bollard you wish to use is already occupied by other mooring ropes slip your rope under those already there – this will permit their owners to depart without disturbing your line.

THE YACHT'S TENDER OR DINGHY

Most cruising yachts will require a small tender at some time or other. It must be well able to support the regular crew safely. Remember that more leisure sailors are drowned from using overloaded dinghies than from other accidents at sea. An inflatable dinghy will support more weight, generally speaking, than a wooden boat of the same size. It also has the added advantage of not harming the mother-ship when tethered alongside – a wooden dinghy in a rough sea can be an agonizing thing to watch.

If a long passage is about to be made and the tender is wooden, then it is best hauled on board and stowed along the coachroof. It should be well lashed down. With an inflatable it can either be partly deflated and similarly stowed or completely deflated and stowed in a convenient locker.

If you are obliged to tow a dinghy then its painter (the line attached to its bows used for securing it) should be a rope with some stretch in it, either nylon or polypropylene. The movement of the mother-vessel under way will cause the painter to jerk and snub and an inflexible rope will inevitably snap.

In smooth sea conditions and with a steady speed, a dinghy can be kept on a reasonably short line astern of the mother-ship. It can even be hauled up tight with only its transom area in the water. However, in bad conditions or when the mother-ship is making erratic progress it should be given a long length of line to prevent it surging under the stern and causing damage. Whatever the conditions it should always be towed centrally behind the mother-ship to avoid excessive drag.

Choosing a Boat

Where choosing a boat is concerned every sailor has his own prejudices. What appears to be ideal for one man is wrong for another and vice versa. The most relevant question to be asked when selecting a sailing boat is: what will she be used for? If the requirement is for a comfortable family cruising boat then her accommodation, handling and performance should be considered with this in mind. If the desire is to race then her speed and handling become the primary concern and her living facilities of secondary importance. Her underwater shape will also greatly affect her performance.

Any prospective purchaser should familiarize himself with as many different types of craft as he can before making an irreversible decision. The variety of craft available is endless, but provided the boat chosen is from a reputable builder, or is one of a well-known class, then it should be a sound investment. It should go without saying that the vessel should also be in good condition, but if there is any doubt about this then money spent on a marine survey is well worthwhile. Today a purchaser has the added advantage of test-sailing one of the many production boats on the market.

An impossible selection to choose from, but there's bound to be one boat that catches your eye.

45

One-Design Class boats. The term 'One-Design' (restricted mainly to boats designed for racing) means that they are required to be as near identical as possible. No individual improvements may be made to enhance the boat's performance.

DINGHIES

The choice within this category seems to grow by the day – like barnacles – but once again it is wise to investigate a varied selection before settling on a specific type.

There are many sailing schools and clubs around the coast where experience can be gained and where instruction is given. The benefits of joining a club or enrolling at a school are that they not only sail well-established, well-known classes but most clubs indulge in regular racing activities as well.

Such classes as the *Enterprise*, *Wayfarer* and the *Mirror* are popular club boats and they are all ideal for family sailing, being both safe and stable, and they also provide excellent sailing for the racing enthusiast.

A dinghy can be used on virtually any stretch of open water – a reservoir, river or the open sea. It is important to note that sailing on the sea, or other tidal waters, is vastly different to sailing on still water. Tidal areas are best

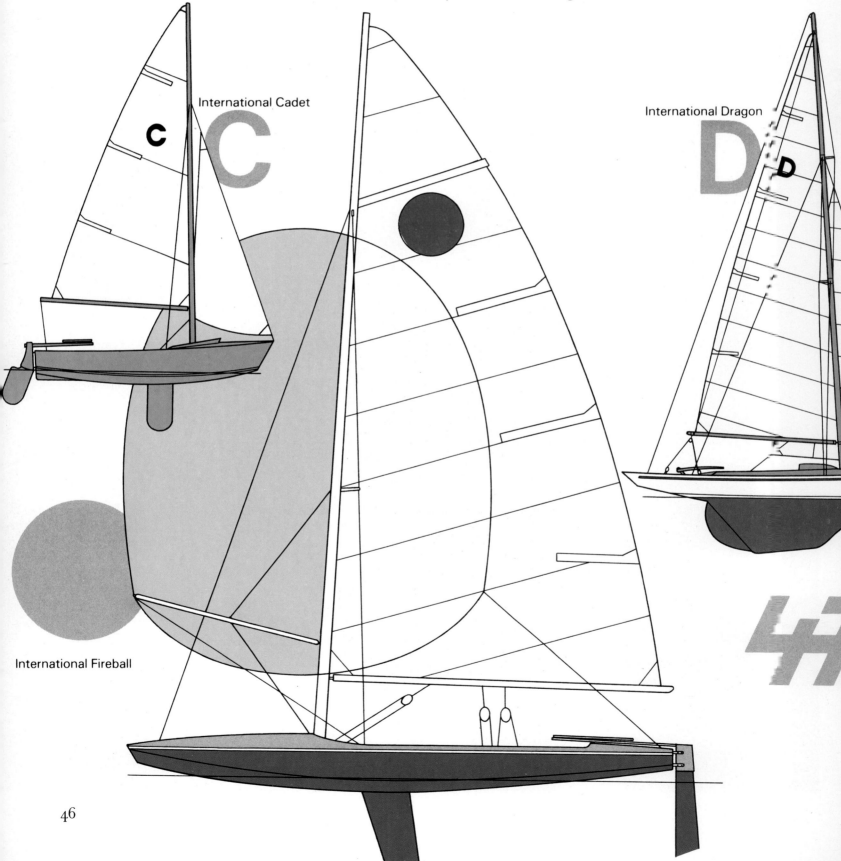

International Cadet

International Dragon

International Fireball

avoided until sufficient experience has been gained.

The sloop-rigged *Wayfarer* has a LOA of 15 feet 10 inches (4·82 metres). She has a large cockpit capable of seating six and has built-in buoyancy at the stern and the bow. Her beam of 6 feet 1 inch (1·85 metres) makes her a very steady boat for use at sea and on rivers and estuaries. Her sail area is not excessive, which allows her to sail in quite a stiff breeze before becoming overpressed. Many Wayfarers have been built of timber construction but the boat is now available with part (hull only) or complete GRP (Glass Reinforced Plastic) construction. Her size and weight prevent her being carried on a roof-rack, but she is easily trailed behind the average car.

The *Mirror* is a very popular class indeed and the numbers built now exceed 5,000. Originally made in kit form, she can still be purchased either for home completion or as a finished boat Smaller than the Wayfarer, the Mirror is 10 feet (3·3 metres) LOA and has a beam of 4 feet 9 inches (1·4 metres); she has the same safe characteristics and a lively performance. She

Good competitive racing can be had in the tried-and-tested Enterprise class.

International 5-0-5

International 470

is easily carried on top of a car and her gunter rig with its short mast can be stowed snugly within the hull during transportation. The Mirror's distinctive red sails are a frequent sight wherever boats abound and she would make an ideal choice as a first boat.

Both the Wayfarer and the Mirror are large enough to be used as overnight campers as a tent can quickly be rigged over the cockpit area. There is room enough inside for two people to sleep and live quite comfortably.

The basic accommodation, or working area, within the average dinghy is usually quite spartan. The cockpit is either fitted with a thwart seat running along each side or else the side decks are extended inboard to allow the crew enough 'bottom' room for sitting comfortably.

A dinghy can heel quite swiftly and it would be fairly precarious for the crew to sit balanced on the edge of the boat without support, so the boats are equipped with stout toe-straps anchored along the cockpit floor. The occupants can hook their toes underneath the straps to lessen the risk of falling out of the boat.

As the need to 'sit out' is essential to maintain balance, the tiller is fitted with an extension arm. This arm is attached to the end of the tiller by a universal joint which permits the helmsman to maintain sensitive steering control while at the same time using his body weight to balance the angle of heel.

Most established dinghy classes have their own Association, and if you are interested in a particular class its representatives will be able to provide any additional information you may require.

PARTS OF A DINGHY

1. mainsail
2. batten pocket
3. boom
4. clew outhaul
5. mainsheet jamming cleat
6. tiller extension
7. tiller
8. spinnaker sheet leads
9. rudder lift line
10. pintle and gudgeon assembly
11. rudder blade
12. toe straps
13. mainsheet traveller control line
14. mainsheet power block
15. mainsheet blocks
15a. mainsheet
16. mainsheet traveller
17. traveller track
18. centreboard case
19. centreboard
20. centreboard control line
21. kicking strap
22. mast step
23. mast
24. mainsail halyard
25. sliding gooseneck
26. luff groove
27. jib
28. forestay
29. bow fitting
30. jib sheets
31. shroud
32. shroud lanyard
33. shroud plate
34. built-in buoyancy

Right: The neat tidy profile of the ever-popular Mirror dinghy.

Below: Pupils from the Cowes Sailing Centre being towed out for morning's tuition in Wayfarers.

A fine example of cruising boat efficiency and luxury – the Bowman 56 – but one requiring a considerably deep pocket.

CRUISERS

Once again the choice available is large, both of old and new boats, but the depth of your pocket could play a slightly more important part in your final choice than it does with a dinghy. The price you pay for a new boat may well stretch your finances to the limit, so it is as well to remember that, unlike a car, a boat will require the addition of many extras before she is safe and ready for sailing.

A good family cruising boat should not only provide a berth for each member of her crew but should also have enough room for them to stow their gear. Far too often a tiny boat is offered as having ample accommodation for six people, but this is usually optimism carried to the extreme. She may well provide a berth for each but it is unrealistic to think of six people *living* on such a small boat, let alone stowing all their personal gear and supplies even for a short trip. Imagine what would happen to her trim if they all sat in the cockpit at the same time; add to that the weight of the engine and her bows would end up pointing to the stars. No, a good cruising boat needs more accommodation than is absolutely necessary for her crew. At sea there should be room to move about freely; congestion leads to confusion, and confusion to carelessness and accidents.

The average cruising boat can be broken down into three separate accommodation areas – the foc'sle (forecabin), the saloon and the cockpit. The foc'sle usually has two berths, one to port and one to starboard, arranged in a vee and tucked into the bows There is often a small chain locker forward of the berths where they meet. Moving aft, the foc'sle is separated from the main saloon by a hanging locker, for oilskins, on one side and a toilet on the other.

In the main saloon the berth numbers may vary but usually there is accommodation for two. It is either arranged as a dinette around a table which when collapsed forms the base for a double bed, or as two single berths, one on each side. The saloon will also house a small galley and an area for navigation with a chart table.

Ideally the galley should be positioned at the rear of the saloon and on the port-hand side close to the companionway steps. In this situation it will receive plenty of ventilation from the main hatch allowing fumes from the cooker to escape. It also means that if a gas cooker is fitted, the supply pipe will have only a short distance to travel from the cockpit cylinder. Lastly, it allows cooking to be done while under way and on the starboard tack with no fear of having to go about halfway through the preparation of a meal. (The starboard tack is the 'right of way' tack, which is explained further in Chapter 5.)

INTERIOR OF A CRUISING BOAT

1. coaming lockers
2. main, sliding hatch
3. fore hatch
4. chain locker
5. shelf
6. forecabin berths
7. toilet compartment
8. clothes locker
9. port berth
10. starboard berth
11. storage
12. companion steps
13. chart table
14. engine
16. keel
17. rudder
18. fuel tank
19. fuel storage
21. galley
22. aft locker hatch

The last area to review is the cockpit. A standard arrangement will have a bench seat on either side. The helmsman can steer from the aft area while the crew sits forward to handle the jib sheets and winches. The cockpit seats are fitted with watertight lids giving access to large stowage lockers beneath. These lockers are ideal for stowing all the boat's warps and fenders where they will be easily accessible when you are preparing to moor. If they are also large enough for the kedge anchor, then so much the better.

Some saloons have a quarter berth which extends below the cockpit area, or even two, and although these are very snug to sleep in while under way their disadvantage is that they prevent the cockpit lockers from being a usable size. Ample locker space within the cockpit area is essential on a well-found vessel. Very often the cockpit runs right back to the transom but sometimes it is terminated a foot or so short to provide an additional stern locker. If there is such a locker on the boat you are examining it is the best place for storing 'smelly' items such as spare cans of fuel and oil – keeping them well way from the living quarters.

The engine is usually situated beneath the cockpit floor, but most modern boats have a watertight self-draining cockpit which leaves access to the engine at the aft end of the saloon behind the companion steps. The self-draining cockpit allows water that has come aboard while sailing to run back into the sea. It escapes through pipes built into the hull at the rear of the cockpit well. These pipes run diagonally from port to starboard and starboard to port and they are steeply angled to prevent any water from re-entering the cockpit.

Safety Afloat

Throughout this book the need for care and attention to detail has been stressed. There is one overriding reason for this – safety. Wherever, or whatever, you sail, it must never be forgotten that the sea is a dangerous place and should never be taken for granted. Safety measures should never be ignored no matter how unnecessary they may seem and no activity should ever be undertaken carelessly – even if you personally are not at risk a thoughtless action on your part could cause danger to others.

RULES OF THE ROAD

It is important to know the basic rules of the road. Unlike road traffic regulations, these should be approached with a degree of flexibility. Occasions will arise when it is prudent to ignore a rule rather than carry on, self-righteously, straight into a collision.

It *was* the rule that power-driven vessels always had to give way to sail. This remains basically true today, but you should use your common sense as well. A small dinghy which stubbornly refuses to take evasive action in front of a large power vessel is just being bloody-minded. It must be remembered that the larger vessel may not have room to manoeuvre within a restricted channel. No pleasure craft, sail or power, should ever force a commercial vessel to take avoiding action.

When two vessels are approaching one another they should take to the starboard side – leaving the other boat to pass down their port-hand side.

A sailing boat with the wind on its starboard side has right of way over a boat with the wind on its port side.

A vessel to windward always gives way to a vessel to leeward.

An overtaking vessel should steer clear of other vessels, irrespective of which tack either vessel is on.

If in doubt of another vessel's intentions, always give him the benefit of the doubt and take evasive action. It is also wise to make your own intentions clear – even to the extent of exaggerating your change of course to make certain that all other craft in the vicinity are aware of what you intend to do.

A little vision and courtesy will go a long way towards safe and pleasant sailing – stubbornness, bravado and one-upmanship have a nasty habit of turning into regret and embarrassment.

It may only be a dummy run in fine conditions but it is well worth the effort. Note the line attaching the liferaft to the mother ship and the harness of the crew in the water securely clipped to it.

A life jacket should easily support the weight of an unconscious body in the water. Many of them, like the one shown here, can be given added buoyancy by air inflation.

SAFETY EQUIPMENT

Generally speaking, personal safety equipment can be limited to life jackets, buoyancy aids and safety harnesses. Whichever piece of equipment you are using two things need to be remembered – the appliance must be in good condition and, most importantly, it must fit. A life jacket is designed to support the weight of an unconscious person in the water, and if it doesn't fit properly it could be washed over the wearer's head.

It is essential to know when a safety aid should be worn, and why. A *life jacket* should always be worn on the following occasions:
1 In any sailing dinghy, no matter how good the weather conditions. Good weather makes people complacent and that's when accidents happen.
2 When travelling to and from a yacht in a tender. Even if the tender is not overloaded, a thoughtless action by a passing power boat could create enough wash to swamp the dinghy and its occupants.
3 When boarding a yacht from a tender. It is foolish for all the occupants to try and disembark together, one person should climb out while the others hold the dinghy steady against the side of the yacht. Don't stand on the edge of the dinghy, use the seat and step up from there. Once all are aboard, the tender should be safely secured.

On a cruiser it is unrealistic to expect every member of the crew to wear a life jacket at all times, but don't let the snugness of the cockpit lull you into a false sense of security. As with a dinghy the times when it is essential to wear a life jacket are as follows:
1 When bad weather is threatened or when it has arrived.
2 When moving round the decks – particularly the foredeck.
3 When preparing to moor – a too-eager leap ashore or a hastily heaved warp could easily end up as a ducking for someone.
4 When the skipper tells you to. This is perhaps the most important of all occasions; there can be only one captain on a boat and if he decides that life jackets are to be worn, then wear them. He more than likely has more experience than you, and although you may feel very overdressed sitting in the sunshine, when the squall hits (the one *you* hadn't seen approaching) you will be glad you took his advice.

If a person does fall overboard then a life jacket will obviously give him support, but if the boat is travelling fast he will soon be left well behind and possibly lost. A *life harness* not only keeps you attached to the boat should you go overboard but can even prevent you going over in the first place. The harness should fit you snugly and feel comfortable; modern harnesses are very strongly made and allow you adequate freedom of movement about the boat, but they should be regularly checked for signs of wear and tear.
A harness should always be worn:
1 In rough weather. Bad conditions can throw a boat about wildly and all the occupants of the cockpit should be securely clipped on.
2 For foredeck work. Changing a headsail often requires the use of both hands, and on a pitching boat a harness will enable you to do the job in comparative safety.
3 Whenever the helmsman is alone in the cockpit, by day or night. In rough weather a large wave could easily lift the stern and tip the helmsman out into the water. If the other members of the crew are down below, it may be some time before the boat's behaviour betrays the helmsman's absence.

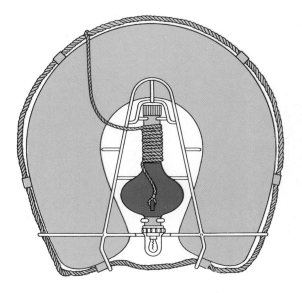

A lifebuoy should always be ready to hand in the area of the boat's cockpit. The light inverted in the centre will automatically switch itself on when floating upright in the water.

Always remember the maxim, 'One hand for the boat and one for you', and wear a harness whenever there is the slightest risk of being thrown overboard. It should be used intelligently and never clipped to anything that is likely to snap or break – always attach the life-line clip to a fixing that is strong enough to withstand the strain imposed on it.

The single most effective piece of safety equipment on a well-found yacht is a good set of *lifelines* or *guard rails*. Some hardy mariners sneer at such refinements and sail around with their treacherous side-decks awash, taking their lives into their hands every time they leave the cockpit. This breed of seaman will only learn the hard way – assuming they are lucky enough to get a second chance.

Lifelines should run completely round the boat, rigged from a strong steel pulpit at the bow and led back through steel stancheon posts to an equally strong pushpit at the stern. They should always be rigged at a sensible height and should never be below knee level. If they are, a sudden backward fall will almost certainly flip you overboard – in fact the low rail will actually tend to help your progress over the side.

Boats are sometimes seen with their lifelines secured with a shackle at the stern and a lashing at the bow. This is wrong; they should always be rigged the other way round. The bow end of the line should be securely shackled and tensioned with a strong lashing at the pushpit, close to the cockpit. In this position any signs of the lashing coming undone or fraying can be quickly remedied.

Although relatively expensive, a *liferaft* should be part of a yacht's standard safety equipment. Even though it may never be used in an emergency it is a wise investment. It should be kept in top-class working order and regularly serviced – most manufacturers will do this for a small fee, and it is money well spent.

A rigid dinghy, even one with built-in buoyancy, is unlikely to withstand a rough night at sea, whereas an *inflatable dinghy* will serve as a good substitute for a proper liferaft. When you purchase an inflatable make sure that it is the type with multiple flotation chambers – then in the event of a puncture in one chamber the others will keep the dinghy afloat.

Always keep a *watertight survival bag* with the liferaft in case the need arises to abandon ship. It should contain a first-aid kit, distress flares and a supply of food and water. If ever you are forced to abandon ship and take to the liferaft, then stay with the 'mother' boat as long as it is safe to do so. Let the dinghy drift away from the boat on a long line but have a knife ready to cut it free should this become necessary. Anyone involved in search and rescue will find it much easier to locate a drifting yacht than a small dinghy which can easily be hidden by the waves. If a liferaft or an inflatable dinghy is carried on the deck it should be securely lashed down, though in such a way that it can be easily released in an emergency.

In addition to a liferaft every yacht should carry at least one *lifebuoy*. It should be attached to a long line and be fitted with a light for use at night. All too often these are mounted on the pushpit – facing outwards! Remember, it is those remaining on board who will be using them, so mount them facing inboard where they are within easy reach.

A good selection of *flares* should be carried at all times; there is a flare for all occasions. The kit should contain hand-held red distress flares for use at night; red smoke flares for use during the daylight hours; red distress rockets or parachute flares for use when far out to sea, or when the visibility is very bad, and finally, white flares for making your position known to other vessels in your vicinity, either at night or in bad visibility. If possible, equip the boat with two sets of flares, one within the cockpit area and one in the saloon. All flares should be stored in waterproof containers and checked regularly to see that their expiry date has not been reached.

Most boats are equipped with an auxiliary engine, either petrol or diesel, and it is the former that is by far the most dangerous. The use of plastic fuel supply pipes should be avoided at all costs; if they are installed close to a hot exhaust pipe, it will only be a matter of time before the boat explodes like a bomb. Fuel pipes should always be copper and arranged so that the fuel runs to port and the exhaust system to starboard, or vice versa. Fuel pipes should be secured at regular intervals to avoid the risk of fracture through vibration. If the supply has a tap at the tank as well as one at the engine,

In rough weather it is sometimes cumbersome to wear both a life jacket and a harness, but when on deck a harness is essential. Here the wearer has passed the line right around the mast before clipping it back to his own belt.

then as an added safeguard switch off your petrol supply at the tank and run the engine to use up the excess fuel remaining in the pipe. *This should only be done with petrol engines and never with a diesel*, or you will cause an airlock rendering the engine useless until the fuel system has been bled to remove it. Petrol fumes are also a danger and both the tank and any spare fuel stored on board should have ample 'breathing space' – the fumes must be allowed to escape freely and disperse into the air.

If a gas cooker is fitted then the supply cylinder should be sited within the cockpit area and preferably stowed in a locker which drains directly overboard or into the self-draining cockpit-well. Cylinder gas is heavier than air (and also odourless) and a small undetected seepage into the main bilge can build up very quickly into a highly explosive mixture. A single spark from a faulty electrical fitting would be more than enough to ignite it and blow the boat to pieces. Gas should be supplied to the cooker through a flexible, armoured steel pipe – never plastic! It should be as short as possible to avoid unnecessary bends and consequent fractures and it should be firmly clamped at each end. One shudders to think of the number of push-on plastic gas pipes to be seen on various boats. On one occasion two boats were seen moored together – one guilty of this fault and one innocent; they burnt from stem to stern and were sunk as charred wrecks in twenty minutes. When you leave a boat always say to yourself, 'GAS OFF! FUEL OFF!'

Place fire extinguishers where they can be easily reached in case of emergency. Don't make the mistake of putting one right next to the cooker, because if the cooker were to catch fire the whole area could easily become a mass of flames and the extinguishers would be out of reach. It is far better to have one on the other side of the saloon, another that can be reached from the forehatch (mounted on the foc'sle bulkhead), and one in the cockpit.

The majority of measures taken in the interests of safety are just simple

There's no sign of panic here — not even a lost hat. They are calmly releasing the sheets before attempting to right the dinghy.

common sense combined with a little care. The engine and the electrical system should be periodically examined and any faults, or even suspected faults, rectified. The rig should be checked for wear and tear and frayed or worn lines either repaired or replaced. A little time and trouble taken at regular intervals will ensure that the boat is always ready and fit for sea.

'MAN OVERBOARD' DRILL

Inevitably all *dinghy* sailors end up in the water. Although this is a common enough occurrence, you should always be on your guard. If you are correctly kitted out with a sound life jacket, then at least you will float. So will the dinghy, as it will not only have its own inherent buoyancy but also its built-in buoyancy – either in the form of watertight chambers in its structure or inflatable bags lashed under the seats. Once in the water the rule is: STAY WITH THE BOAT!

Never attempt to swim to the shore. It may look close but appearances can be very deceptive at sea. Even in summer waters it won't take long for the body to become chilled and this is soon followed by exhaustion. The chances of reaching the shore are reduced and you will be possibly putting yourself and would-be rescuers at risk.

When a capsize occurs – don't panic, even if you find youself smothered by the sails. Swim out from under and straight away make for the sheets to free them. If you can, try to manoeuvre the boat so that she heads into the wind. Then make your way round the dinghy so that you are behind the upturned hull. Stand on the centre-board and take hold of the edge of the boat as high as you can reach, stretch up and lean out to lever the boat back into an upright position. As the dinghy will probably be quite full of water, don't climb in over the side or you may capsize her the other way on top of you; make your way round to the stern and climb in over the transom.

If you are not alone, your crew will have to remain in the water until you have bailed out enough water to give the boat the buoyancy to support you both. When this has been done, the person in the water can also climb in over the transom.

By the way – where's the rudder? Most dinghy rudders are simply dropped into place prior to casting off; if you want to keep yours after a capsize secure it to the boat with a lanyard.

If someone goes overboard from a *cruiser* then the following rescue procedure should be carried out to the letter – and carried out fast! Don't break the rules or a mishap could very quickly turn into a disaster.

Immediately someone goes overboard a crew member should try to maintain visual contact. It is surprisingly easy to lose sight of a bobbing head even in a relatively calm sea. Simultaneously a lifebuoy should be thrown as close to the person in the water as possible. Throw it *close to*, not *at* him – a stunned or unconscious subject will be more difficult to rescue.

If you are under sail, whether beating, running or reaching, you must immediately *gybe*. This is without question the quickest way of putting the boat about and making a return run to execute a rescue. If only one person remains on board, then of course all this will need to be done single-handed, *and* a watch kept on the person in the water at the same time.

The engine should be started to aid your manoeuvrability as you head back towards the person in the water. Take care as you make your final approach and always:

1 Approach from the leeward side.
2 Watch your propellor.

If the approach is made from upwind you risk running the person down. He will be drawn under the boat and possibly drowned. There is no need to go into details about the possible effects of the propellor should a careless approach be made.

As you draw near, a line can be thrown and once the person in the water has a good hold and is well secured, the engine can be cut and the sails dropped. The person can now be lifted aboard and, assuming he is not injured, the best medicine is a change into warm dry clothes, a hot drink and plenty of rest.

The good sailor will practise the 'man overboard' procedure before it becomes a reality. It is much safer to know what needs to be done in advance than to find yourself in an emergency and powerless to help.

Boat Maintenance

A little neglect goes a long way. If the small routine jobs are put off, they soon become major operations. Remember the old saying, 'A stitch in time saves nine'. It applies perfectly to the maintenance of a boat.

A vessel and her gear are at constant risk from the ravages of the elements and, if she is to give good service, she must be well protected – at all times! Most of the boats built today are of Glass Reinforced Plastic (GRP), which has largely replaced the use of timber as the standard boat-building material. Its advantages over timber are that it is lighter in weight yet still retains the necessary strength to withstand the power of the sea. Also, hulls can be built much more quickly. What is more, the quality of timber required for boat-building needs to be superlative: the preparatory stages involve careful selection, storage and lengthy seasoning, and make it a very expensive material. Add to this the scarcity of shipwrights with the necessary skill for building in wood, and it is not difficult to understand why GRP is now so popular.

METHODS OF CONSTRUCTION WITH GRP

Building with GRP requires, initially, the construction of a wooden hull known as a *plug*, and its exterior needs to be very highly finished. The surface is sanded smooth and polished to remove all imperfections and blemishes before being coated with a sealing agent. GRP is then laid up on the outside of the plug to produce a 'female' mould. After curing (hardening), it is removed as two separate halves and polished to remove any flaws from the inside surface. The mould is strongly braced to retain the correct shape of the boat, and is now ready to be used for the production of the actual hull.

Next, glass strand matting, impregnated with epoxy resin, is laid up in successive layers inside the mould until the correct hull thickness is achieved. Strengthening members for deck fittings, engine bearers, etc., are glassed into the structure as the work progresses. When the hull has completely

A gleaming new hull is released from its mould. Note the removable panels in the mould which are necessary to extract the bilge keels.

A busy boat shed with wooden hulls in various stages of completion – from almost finished to the early 'skeleton' on the right.

cured, the mould, which has previously been treated with a releasing agent, is split and the finished hull exposed. The shell is fairly floppy so the main bulkheads and the deck are bonded into place. The hull is now ready for fitting out, and many boats are sold at this stage for home completion.

Sandwich construction is an alternative to the conventional method of building with GRP. It is suitable for building large hulls for which extreme lightness and strength are needed. The sandwich method uses no mould and has a slightly different type of plug. This is not highly finished but is a very accurate contoured wooden framework. Expanded polystyrene foam sheet or balsa wood is then folded round the framework and glass mat laid up all over it. When this has cured the part-built hull is released and a second layer of glass laid up on the inside; the foam or balsa is thus sandwiched between the two layers of glass. As with the conventional method, the hull is strengthened where required.

METHODS OF CONSTRUCTION WITH TIMBER

A wooden boat is constructed by exterior planking attached in various ways to a complex inner framework or skeleton. The main construction methods are *clinker* (or clench), *carvel*, *cold-moulded* and *hard chine*.

Clinker construction has the longitudinal planking overlapped. By means of copper nails each plank is clenched (riveted) to its neighbour and through to the framework.

Carvel construction has the planking laid up edge to edge with each plank securely fastened to the frame. This method results in a hull with a smooth exterior as opposed to the lapped effect of a clinker boat.

Moulded hulls are built over a skeleton mould using thin layers of veneer glued diagonally from keel to deck edge. Alternate layers of veneer are laid at right angles to each other, and as the glue cures on one layer so the next is applied until the necessary thickness is built up. Despite their strength, moulded hulls are difficult for the amateur to repair, and if damaged will need professional attention.

The last method of timber construction, hard chine, is probably the simplest for the amateur builder to tackle. The interior framework is fabricated as straight-sectioned angled frames assembled along the keel, and it is then covered with a skin of marine-quality plywood to form the hull.

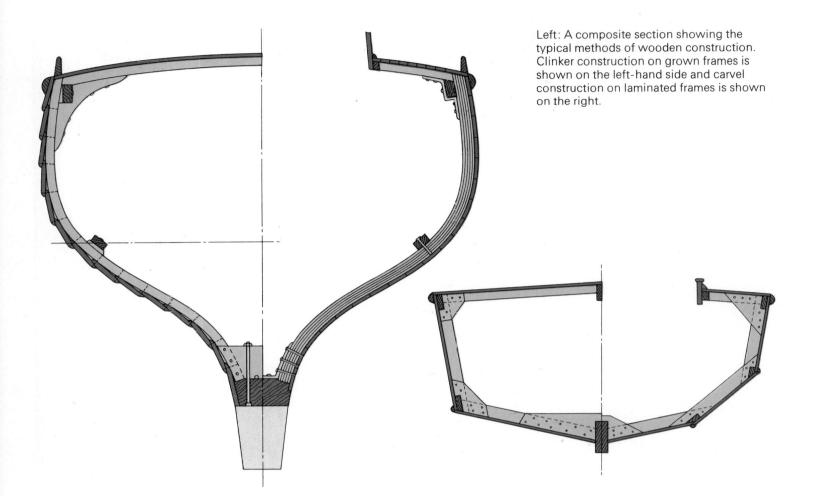

Left: A composite section showing the typical methods of wooden construction. Clinker construction on grown frames is shown on the left-hand side and carvel construction on laminated frames is shown on the right.

Plywood does not have a facility for double curvature and will only bend successfully within one plane. This results in a hull curve created by a series of flats. The point where two of these flats meet along the line of the hull is called the chine – hence the name of the method.

As well as hard-chine building with plywood, boat-frame timber may be either 'grown', i.e. cut from a conveniently shaped living tree; laminated, with thin pieces of wood glued together and bent around a pre-formed jig; or steam-bent, in which process the timber is steamed under pressure and then while still hot bent around a jig. It is allowed to cool while clamped in place, and when released it retains the shape of the jig.

Whether you are dealing with GRP or wood it is advisable to spend some time finding out how your boat is constructed (assuming you did not build her yourself!). The more you know about her the more you will know what to look for in the event of trouble, and the more you will be able to care for her.

GENERAL CARE - FINISH

The surface of all GRP boats has an outer skin called a *gel coat*. This, to a large extent, protects it from the elements but not from the wear and tear of careless seamanship. The gel coat must be well looked after, and dirt and stains, especially oil and petrol which will discolour the surface, should be washed off regularly with a mild detergent solution. Careful boat handling will avoid unnecessary scuffs and scrapes. When they do occur, these can be quite easily polished out with a gentle abrasive such as metal polish. After polishing, the area should be washed clean.

GRP is not, as is commonly thought, waterproof. Therefore, to prevent water penetration, minor abrasions and scratches should be repaired as soon as possible. Deeper scratches should be thoroughly cleaned to remove any dirt or grease and then a matching gel solution painted into the scratch, if necessary building up with several layers of gel until the right thickness is reached. Cover the repair with polythene sheeting taped firmly all round to allow the gel to cure properly away from the atmosphere; finally it should be burnished down to blend with the surrounding area. When major damage is sustained it is advisable to seek professional advice before attempting amateur repairs.

Timber has only three basic finishes – paint, varnish, and natural or raw.

Above: This section clearly shows the flat appearance of hard-chine building – single chine on the left and double chine on the right.

The detail below shows the overlapping veneers of moulded construction.

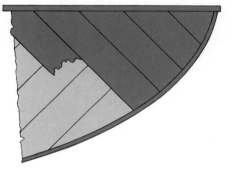

The majority of wooden boats are painted, and surface damage can be
repaired as with any other painted wooden item, but the best-quality
materials should always be used and the preparatory work should never be
skimped. Exposed timber should be first treated with a clear preservative,
then a primer (aluminium), then an undercoat, and finished with a top-coat
of good-quality marine gloss.

Most boats have some varnish work, or 'brightwork' as it is called, and if
regularly inspected it can easily be kept in good condition. At the first sign of
any wear or damage the affected area should be rubbed down with fine
sandpaper and new varnish *of the same type* applied. It should be built up in
layers until the repair matches the surrounding area, each successive layer
being lightly rubbed down between coats.

If the damage is such that you need to rub down to bare wood then one
or two coats of varnish, diluted in equal parts with white spirit, should be
applied before full-strength varnish is used to finish off. The diluted mixture
allows the varnish to soak well into the timber, so giving a very good base for
the final coats. New timber should always be treated in this way, the diluted
solution being applied with a soft cloth pad and rubbed right into the grain
of the wood. This treatment also brings out the natural colour of the wood.

If brightwork gets chipped, particularly polyurethane, it is wise to repair
it as quickly as possible. Unlike conventional varnish this type does not seem
to sink into the timber so deeply, but tends to form a skin on the surface. If
this skin is accidentally broken, damp will penetrate, loosen the varnish and
fade the colour as it spreads out from the damaged area.

The only raw timber one should see on a boat is teak – it has an abundant
quantity of natural oil and can safely be left untreated and exposed. The
elements will eventually cause it to lose its colour and turn it a silky grey.
However, a periodic rub down will return it to its original colour. Like other
timbers teak can be varnished, but because of its density and oil content the
varnish needs to penetrate very deeply to achieve a lasting finish.

LOOKING FOR TROUBLE

Although GRP does not rot it is still prone to attack, and when trouble starts
it is advisable to take immediate action. Examine the hull closely for signs of
failure on the gel coat. Any hairline cracks discovered should be filled or
they will permit water to enter the lay of the glass – this will eventually
spread out and badly damage the hull. A star-shaped crack usually indicates

an impact fracture and both the inside and the outside of the hull should be checked to ascertain the extent of the damage.

The area below the waterline should receive particular attention and if any evidence of blistering is found professional advice should be sought without delay. Blisters could be the first signs of osmosis, and if so the hull will suffer a high degree of water penetration unless prompt action is taken. All the through-deck fittings should be looked at to see that they are not working loose, thus imposing excessive strains on the skin and causing additional cracks.

Wooden boats, by contrast, do rot: not, as might be expected, from sea water, but from fresh water. Every effort should be made to ensure that the boat is well covered when she is left on her mooring unattended. If rain water is allowed to lie on the decks it will seep into the timber and eventually the wood will start to rot. In the old days when a boat was launched she was filled with sea water and large amounts of block-salt were then added to 'pickle her'. The method worked, so if fresh water does find its way into the bilges, flush it out immediately with ample quantities of sea water.

Sound wood, if tapped with a hammer, will give a hard ringing tone in reply. If it is rotten the answering note will be dead and spongy. The only positive cure for rot is to cut out the affected area until sound timber is reached. If it is found within the main structure of the boat it is best to seek the help of a shipwright before taking up your saw and perhaps unwittingly cutting too far into a cricital member.

If wood becomes soft because of water absorption it can sometimes be restored by soaking it with linseed oil. Surround the soft area with a plastic sheet securely taped in place, in such a way that the oil forms a small reservoir. It can then slowly seep into the wood over a period of time. If the wood remains soft after this treatment, the trouble should be regarded as rot and the affected area cut away.

GALVANIC ACTION

Unfortunately there is not room enough in this book to cover the complexities of this subject – of noble metals versus ignoble metals – but it should be noted that the metal fittings on a vessel have their own peculiar form of rot. Some metals are incompatible with others and, when introduced into a salt-laden atmosphere, with water acting as the catalyst, they are subject to what is known as galvanic, or electrolytic action. For this reason all metal fittings should be given regular attention and expert advice sought to establish the specific protection needed for your vessel.

MASTS AND SPARS

Modern spars made from anodized aluminium require little maintenance other than the occasional wash-down with a mild detergent solution to remove the everyday stains of wind and weather. All the fittings should be checked for signs of strain and for any rivets that might have pulled loose.

Wooden masts and spars, however, demand a closer examination. Any cracks that are found could reduce the strength of the spar; they should be filled to prevent water penetration. Rot is very often found close to the fittings, particularly those that are through-bolted, so these also should be examined regularly.

LAYING UP

During the late autumn and winter months many boats are taken ashore and laid up, or stored – either inside a dry shed or out in the open in a boat-yard. While this precaution will protect them from the ravages of a sea berth, it is still necessary to take steps to ensure their safety.

As the boat leaves the water, all the weed and barnacles should be thoroughly washed off with fresh water. She is then blocked up off the ground and stoutly braced with timber supports. Many GRP production boats have their own specially designed cradles which are ideal for this purpose.

At this stage it is a good idea to spend some time making a list of all the things that need doing. Working from stem to stern, note down all the essential jobs and any improvements you may want to put in hand. Try not to leave everything to the last minute in the hope of a bright spring. Start

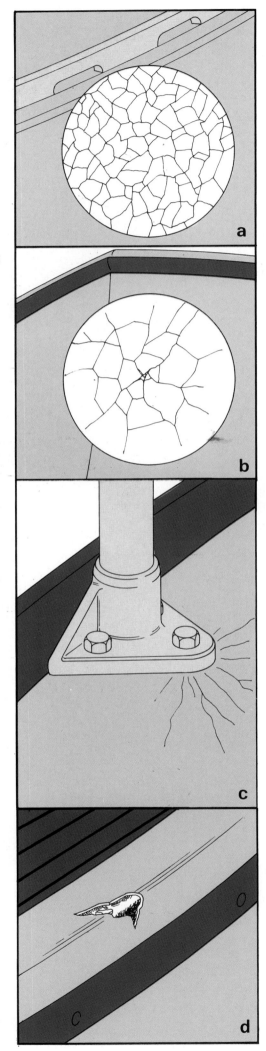

Not, perhaps, a permanent winter berth but still a nicely snugged-down boat securely protected from most of the elements. A better arrangement would have included the addition of breast ropes.

straight away and shorten the work list before winter sets in.

With a wooden hull apply priming paint to any exposed wood to protect it from frost. With a GRP hull apply a thick coating of wax polish (not one with a silicone base), and leave it to give ample protection during the winter; in the spring it can be washed off with all the dirt and grime that would otherwise have attacked the gel coat.

Remove as much portable gear as possible from the boat and store it where it will be safe and dry. The engine should be 'winterized' according to the manufacturer's instructions, and any other mechanical equipment should be serviced and oiled. The ship's battery should be removed and checked before re-charging. If the sails need attention, or are soiled, they should be despatched for overhaul and laundering.

Stainless-steel wire rigging should be washed in warm soapy water and then thoroughly rinsed. Galvanized wire can be treated with a solution of raw linseed oil diluted with petrol which will prolong its useful working life. Never twist rigging wire or it may kink and become seriously weakened; always coil it loosely and tie it to secure the free ends.

Finally, protect the boat from the weather with a waterproof cover. This can either be made of canvas or reinforced plastic sheeting. Avoid using polythene – even the strongest grade will flap itself to pieces in a gale and leave the vessel exposed. The winter months, with their frequent heavy frosts, are the most damaging to a boat and it is worth investing in the best-quality cover you can afford. It should be rigged to allow air to circulate freely throughout the boat, allowing it to breathe and stay fresh. If the boat is too tightly wrapped up, condensation will occur and cause mildew. Before the cover is finally lashed down all round, any deck fittings that may penetrate or chafe it should be well padded.

Work can continue throughout the winter, some being done at home and some on board. The hull can be prepared well in advance of the next season, and you then need only apply a coat of anti-fouling before launching. It is always rewarding to wake up in the spring to find that most of the jobs on your list have been completed. Start work early and it will not be long before you are once more in the water – and sailing.

Navigation

The two lines of men shivered in the cold as they rested on their heavy oars; slowly the great longship drifted to a stop on the quiet surface of the sea. All around them was a circular wall of mist and they strained their eyes to pierce the gloom. They had not seen the sun for seven days – they were lost.

In the stern, close to the huge steering oar, stood a tall figure clad from head to foot in thick furs. The icy air gnawed at his drawn cheeks and he drew the fur closer about his throat. His exhausted men looked up expectantly towards him as he stooped and took a grey dove from a small willow cage. Raising his arm high he set it free into the cold air. The bird flew up and settled on the high carved prow of the boat, then flapping into the air again it circled above their heads – once, twice, finally it turned and flew off into the gloom far away on the starboard bow.

The chief smiled quietly to himself and pointed after the bird. 'It's going home,' he said softly to the helmsman beside him. The men stirred and pulled hard on the oars to bring the longship on to its new course. Soon, as they rowed, the mist cleared and in the distance they could see snow-capped mountains rising over the horizon.

Apart from the sun the Vikings had little to aid them as they travelled across the oceans of the world. The science of navigation had not been born, its complexities and tabular calculations were as yet undiscovered and the vagaries of the earth's magnetism were still a mystery.

Columbus, Magellan, and even Cook on his earlier voyages navigated more by luck than judgment – their charts unconfirmed, their compasses primitive and their instruments unwieldy and very often inaccurate. First, by using a quadrant and later with a cross-staff, they determined their position of latitude but it was not until the invention of the chronometer, making accurate time-checks possible, that a position of longitude could be established.

Eventually the mystery became a science and, like most sciences, it is

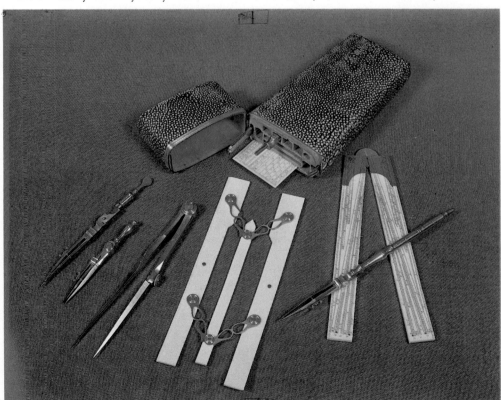

A set of drawing instruments as used by the map makers of the 18th century.

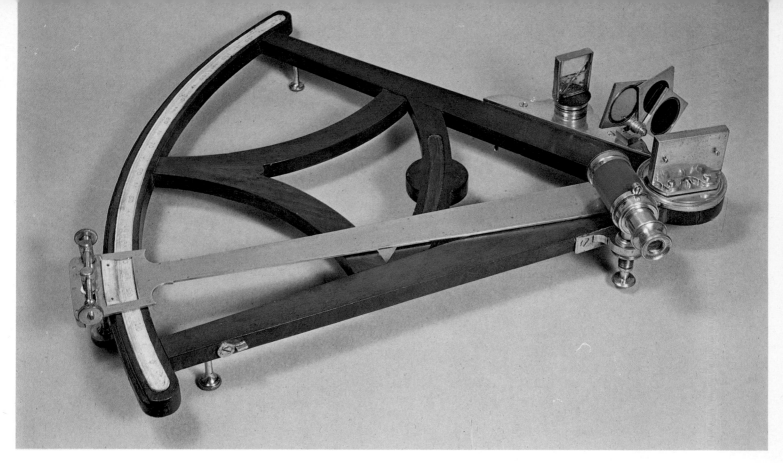

Above: A finely made early sextant, advanced in its time but primitive by the high technology of today's navigational aids.

governed by simple rules that must be followed. Many books have been devoted to navigation, and for those seriously interested in sailing a study course, or further reading on the subject, is essential. A word of warning, though: no one should ever attempt to sail beyond the limits of his navigational knowledge.

THE MAGNETIC COMPASS

Man has known of the earth's magnetic field for centuries and was well aware of the value of the compass. However, one fact that he was not aware of was that the compass does not point towards True North, to the Arctic Pole, but to a position close to it known as Magnetic North. This magnetic position varies throughout the year over a radius of fifty miles around the True Pole; this *variation* must be accounted for when navigational calculations are computed.

The magnetic compass is not only affected by the earth's magnetism, it is also subject to the influence of adjacent ferrous metal. When a compass is installed in a vessel the effect of this influence must be tabulated and compass readings corrected accordingly. This is known as compass *deviation*, and it is interesting to speculate where Columbus would have unwittingly ended up had there been an iron cannon mounted close to his compass.

Explorers of the past also had no accurate way of measuring the speed of their boats through the water, or the exact distance travelled. Nowadays these figures can be obtained from a ship's *log*, an instrument which not only measures the speed of the vessel but also records the distance travelled. With a knowledge of the direction steered, the time taken and a measured distance, plus an allowance made for deviation and variation, a position can be fixed. But is it that simple? No. We have already discussed in Chapter 2 the effect of leeway (the sideways movement of a boat through the water caused by the pressure of the wind on it). The amount of leeway incurred will also need to be included in navigational calculations. But a factor with an even greater influence on the course made good (the actual direction achieved by the vessel) is the tide.

A modern grid compass equipped with a night reading light and set in gymbals.

TIDES AND CURRENTS

The tides and currents of the oceans are ever-changing – in direction, time and strength. The influence of the moon and the sun pull the waters of the earth this way and that. Although seemingly inconsistent, the tides have been carefully measured and the time of high and low water, together with the rise and fall, recorded and tabulated for every day of the year.

Their direction and strength (speed over the sea-bed) have been charted and calculated from known high-water times taken at specific reference ports all around the coastlines of the world. Sailing close to one of these tidal reference ports (known as Standard Ports), you will be able to work out from Tide Tables and from a Tidal Stream Atlas what effect the tide will have on any course you choose to set. A time allowance, either plus or minus, is always specified for other ports in the adjacent area of the Standard Port.

When the moon and sun are in conjunction, or diametrically opposed, the strongest pull is exerted – the tides run fast and high and are known as *springs*. As the moon wanes the tides slow down or 'fall off', their rise and fall also decreases – these tides are called *neaps*. At the lowest point of the neap range the tide will begin to 'make' again towards springs, the whole cycle taking about one calendar month to complete.

Knowing the exact state of the tide, therefore, will have a marked effect on the progress of a voyage. If you set sail with a knowledge of the tides and let the tide work for you, the duration of the passage can be halved. There is little satisfaction in doing the reverse and punching a foul tide for hours and hours – a tired and frustrated crew will often take unwise decisions from motives of expediency, and this can make matters even worse.

CHARTS

Only one more requirement is necessary for successful navigation – a chart. Modern charts are very carefully prepared and give a very accurate picture of the sea in any particular area. A 'compass rose', marked with True North and Magnetic North, will be placed somewhere on the chart together with details of the annual increase or decrease in magnetic variation.

Inset charts, relevant to harbours and ports shown on the base chart, are often featured and the greater detail of their larger scale will give special help to the sailor finding his way into a strange port. Many charts also give tidal-stream information and time differences from the nearest Standard Port of reference. Soundings (depths) are marked all over the chart and these have been recorded at, or just below, the Mean Low Water Spring (MLWS) level. This level is known as the *chart datum* and is based on the lowest expected tide predicted from existing records. Sandbanks that are uncovered at low water but could be a hazard when covered are also shown, with their drying height above the datum level clearly marked – the figures in this instance are always underlined.

As with land maps, charts show clear contour lines for various depths. These can often be useful for fixing a vessel's position when regular soundings are taken. Magellan, groping his way through the Cape Straits, was forced constantly to heave a lead and line to ascertain his depth. A modern electronic echo-sounder will bounce a radio signal off the sea bed and record the exact depth at the flick of a switch.

Above: The traditional lead and line was marked along its length with tags at known points to determine the depth of water.

Left: A diagram showing the tidal range between its highest rise and its lowest fall.

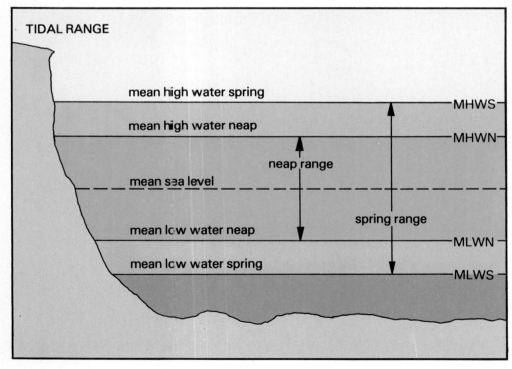

TIDAL RANGE

mean high water spring — MHWS

mean high water neap — MHWN

neap range

mean sea level

spring range

mean low water neap — MLWN

mean low water spring — MLWS

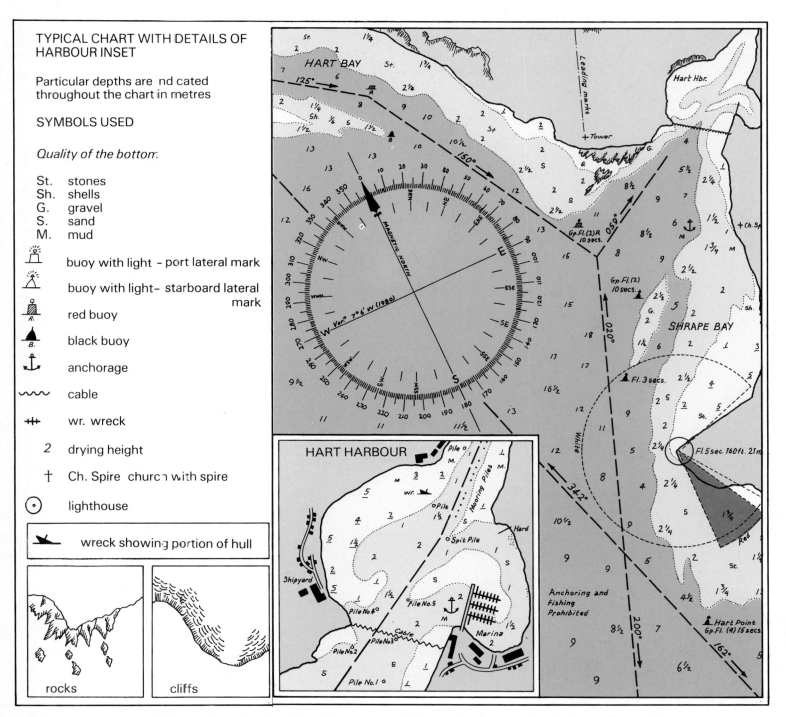

TYPICAL CHART WITH DETAILS OF HARBOUR INSET

Particular depths are indicated throughout the chart in metres

SYMBOLS USED

Quality of the bottom:

St. stones
Sh. shells
G. gravel
S. sand
M. mud

buoy with light – port lateral mark

buoy with light – starboard lateral mark

red buoy

black buoy

anchorage

cable

wr. wreck

2 drying height

† Ch. Spire church with spire

lighthouse

wreck showing portion of hull

rocks   cliffs

Charts also give details of the nature of the sea-bed – whether it is sand, gravel, mud, rocks or weed. There will also be warnings about any dangers in the area such as isolated rocks, wrecks, heavy overfalls (upward currents which can seriously disturb the water in bad weather), and tide races, where opposing currents meet. Other navigational features such as buoys, lighthouses and radio beacons will have their positions marked, each with an accurate (but abbreviated) description of its colour and light characteristics. The positions of these buoys are sometimes changed to accommodate the shift of sand banks which are notorious for catching the unwary mariner. So never sail with an out-of-date chart.

With all this information calculated, tabulated, charted and plotted, and with modern instruments such as radio direction finders, radar, sextants, chronometers, echo-sounders and all manner of electronic extras, the world might seem a small and unexciting place to explore. Assuredly, it is not. Even so, how different it would be to set sail, as our forbears did, with perhaps only a primitive compass and a hand-drawn chart. One can imagine they felt much as sailors still do today when their small ships forged their way through heavy seas under a press of sail.

But would any of us really be brave enough to set sail for unknown lands with a chart that marked the ends of the world with the awesome words, 'Here be Dragons'?

Although geographically make-believe, the chart above gives a good example of the variety of information found on a typical navigational chart.

Introduction
to Boardsailing

At the height of the surfing boom centred on the Californian coast of the United States a group of surfers lazed on the beach watching the breeze ruffle the surface of the oily swells. A few optimistic surfers paddled their boards out to sea in the hope that a larger roller might stray their way. Meanwhile the newly designed surf catamarans utilized the breeze to whisk their excited crews backwards and forwards across the waves.

One of the watchers was Jim Drake and he began to wonder how a surf board could be adapted to carry a sailing rig.

As an experienced sailor he understood the mechanical limitations of the surf board and the considerable stresses set up by the conventionally supported mast and sail. His answer was simplicity itself – remove the stresses altogether by attaching the mast to the board with a universally pivoting joint and use the sailor as the support for the mast and sail. After various experiments he enlisted the financial support of Hoyle Schweitzer and a patent was drawn up. Eventually the patent rights passed to Schweitzer and the Windsurfer Class was born and brought into limited production.

Interest remained lukewarm until a group of Europeans brought the windsurfer to the open beaches of the North Sea. In particular, the Germans and Dutch took to the sport in a very big way creating a demand which necessitated the establishment of a European factory.

Bob Bond

Development of Boardsailing

To understand why, in the space of ten years, a completely new chapter has been written in sailing history it is necessary to look at the attractions of boardsailing. By far the greatest is the fact that the boardsailor becomes an integral part of the sailing vehicle; it is an extension of his body and his senses requiring the same skills of balance and dexterity as a skater or a skier. Additionally, because of the board's compact size and light weight it is easily stowed on the top of a car – or even carried on to aircraft as hand luggage, enabling the boardsailor to choose the most suitable venue for each day's sailing.

The cost of a board can be as little as one-third of the cost of a one-man dinghy such as the International Laser. Low cost alone has opened up sailing to millions who would otherwise have rejected it. Unlike most other forms of sailing there is no need to join a club in order to park your boat when you are not using it – instead the board can be stowed at home against a wall or under the garage roof, ready for immediate use.

Finally, the portability of the board enables boardsailors to utilize every available public water, irrespective of its size. In Northern Europe and the Mediterranean this very portability has brought chronic congestion to many inland lakes and waterways to such an extent that some waters may be prohibited to boardsailors in the interests of safety to navigation by other water users.

COMPONENT PARTS

Since the introduction of the original Windsurfer literally hundreds of designs have been produced by other manufacturers. This has led to complicated legal battles between the patent holder and unlicensed manufacturers and may have a bearing on the Olympic future of this branch of sailing.

The original concept has remained remarkably unchanged and all sailboards share the same basic design features.

The *board* is normally around 4 m (13 feet) in length and can be made of any material. There are two different families of boards – the flat board which is ideal for beginners and general recreation, and the round board

Preceding page: A Windglider riding the Hawaiian surf.

Racing: IYRU Division II (round boards).

70

which is much more difficult to sail and is a racing board. 'Flat' and 'round' refer to the shape of the underside of the board; as a rough guide if it looks like a plank it's a 'flat' board but if it has a boat-shaped hull it's a 'round' board. Specialized boards are manufactured for wave jumping and freestyle sailing, but these should be regarded as the Grand Prix machines and are strictly for experts.

The *skeg* or fin is fitted to the underside of the back of the board. Always keep a spare in case of damage.

The *dagger/centreboard* is the retractable foil housed in a slot on the centreline just aft of the mast attachment point. Daggerboards move vertically – centreboards are pivoted and usually retract into a recess in the board. Both are controlled with the feet.

The *sail* is triangular with a sleeve along its leading edge to accommodate the mast. A slot is cut into the sleeve so that the wishbone booms can be attached to the mast. There are four basic sizes for sails:

$6\,m^2$ ($64 \cdot 5\,ft^2$) for racing
$5\,m^2$ ($54\,ft^2$) for recreation sailing
$4\,m^2$ ($43\,ft^2$) for storm sails
$3\,m^2$ ($32\,ft^2$) for teaching in strong winds.

Overleaf: The transition to strong winds. The body has to be well outboard to counteract the pull of the rig.

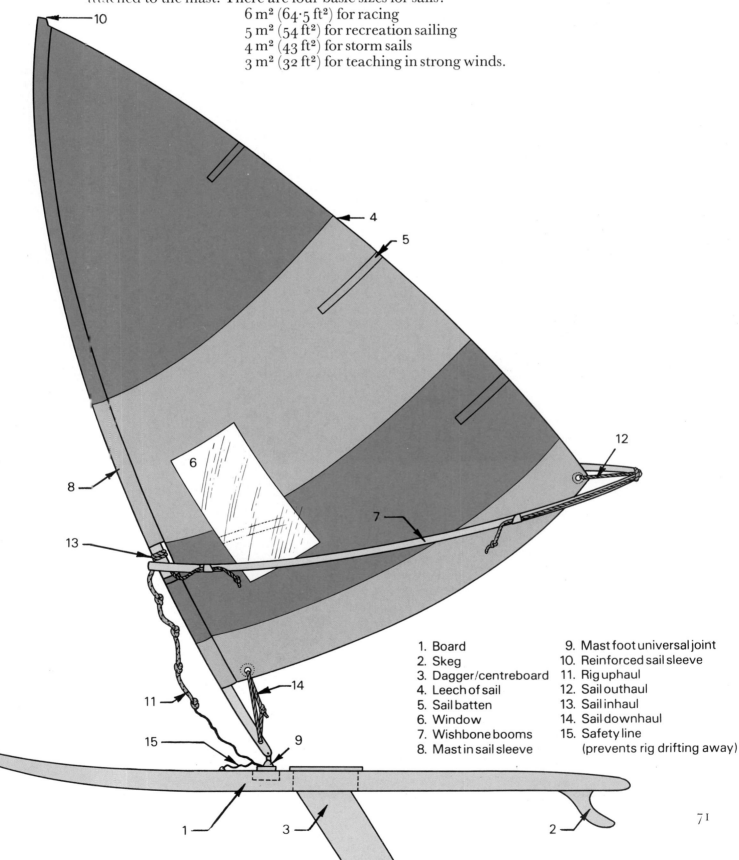

1. Board
2. Skeg
3. Dagger/centreboard
4. Leech of sail
5. Sail batten
6. Window
7. Wishbone booms
8. Mast in sail sleeve
9. Mast foot universal joint
10. Reinforced sail sleeve
11. Rig uphaul
12. Sail outhaul
13. Sail inhaul
14. Sail downhaul
15. Safety line
(prevents rig drifting away)

71

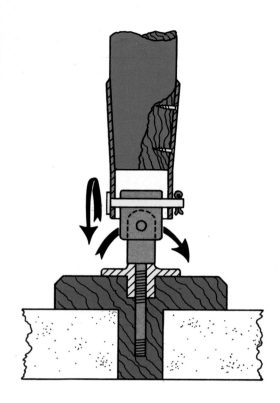

The mast pivot enables the rig to move in any direction above the board.

Sails should be thought of as the gears on a car which enable the engine to run within a limited range of revolutions. Different sail sizes enable the boardsailor to match his/her strength and fitness to a wide range of wind speeds. When you first start to sail the best combination is a 5 m² (54 ft²) sail and a storm sail. The trailing edge – the *leech* – is sometimes stiffened with *battens*. Most sails are fitted with clear plastic *windows* which enable the boardsailor to see other water users.

The *mast* is made either of aluminium or plastic. It is designed to flex, especially in gusty conditions.

The *mast pivot* is a universal swivelling device of metal or plastic which enables the rig to move in any direction above the board. It usually incorporates a friction quick-release device which frees the rig from the board in a violent capsize. The rig should always be attached to the board with a *safety line*.

The *wishbone boom* encompasses the sail. It is attached to the forward edge of the mast with a lashing. The back corner – *clew* – of the sail is attached to the outboard ends of the wishbones by a lashing or adjustable control line – *outhaul* – which varies the flatness of the sail when it is set.

The *uphaul* is a thick rope attached to the forward end of the wishbone boom at its upper end and to the mast foot by means of thin shock cord. Its purpose is to enable the rig to be raised from the water to a sailing position.

The *downhaul* is used to tension the leading edge – *luff* – of the sail. The inter-relationship of the downhaul and outhaul determine whether the sail is flat or full for strong and light winds respectively.

ASSEMBLING THE BOARD AND RIG

When you come to assemble your own or a school's board you may find some variations on the basic method listed here. This is because manufacturers constantly update their products and find new ways of attaching the various component parts. Most new boards come complete with a set of instructions.

The Board The board itself is usually complete. The skeg is attached in its housing with catches or, more usually, machine screws. Once fitted, most sailors leave it permanently attached.

Dagger or centreboards are usually removed in transit and replaced prior to launching. When the board is parked prior to launching it is customary to use the daggerboard to prop the board on its side at an angle of 45° so that the skeg is kept clear of the ground.

The safety/towing line is attached to the towing eye and led back to the mast foot ready to be clipped to the rig when you launch.

The Rig The complete rig comprises the mast and mast pivot, the sail, the wishbone booms and the uphaul line. Once assembled they form a complete single unit – the rig.

The mast, incorporating the mast foot, is usually sealed to prevent its sinking. The sail has a sleeve at its forward edge to accommodate the mast. The wishbone booms are attached to the forward edge of the mast with a lashing of thin rope and the sail is tensioned between the booms with either a lashing or control lines.

One thing is certain, you will have to learn one or two 'knots', properly called bends and hitches, before you can go afloat.

The Inhaul Knot The rope which attaches the booms to the mast is often called the *inhaul*. The simplest method of attaching the rope to the mast is first to tie a stopper knot in one end. Form a loop and pass it around the mast, tuck the knot and the long end of the rope through the loop and tighten so that the knot rests firmly against the mast. Attach the boom to the mast with the long end of the rope.

Rolling Hitch An alternative to the inhaul knot is the rolling hitch. Take two complete turns around the mast then pass the free end up and over the turns, passing it back through the loop formed. Secure the end with a simple hitch. Tighten the turns to form a compact non-slip hitch. In slippery ropes it helps to put a stopper knot in the end. The pull should always be away from the final hitch.

Bowline It sometimes helps to fix a loop in the end of a lashing to enable you to use it as a purchase to gain a mechanical advantage. The simplest is a bowline, formed as illustrated on page 43.

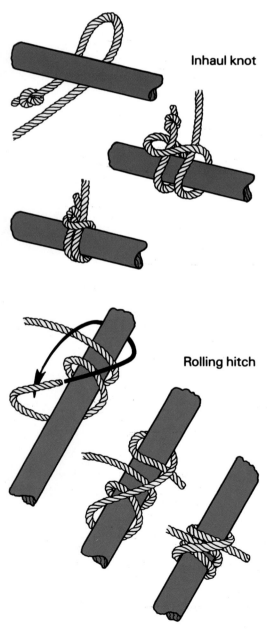

Inhaul knot

Rolling hitch

Learning to Boardsail

Above: Launching the assembled rig and board – an alternative to rigging the board afloat.

Below: Raising the rig from the water.
Sail in the starting position.
Correct hand position.
Gripping the wishbone boom in the cross hands position.
Rig pulled forward, back hand shoulder width behind front hand.

By far the simplest and quickest way to learn how to handle the board is to attend a reputable boardsailing school which has trained, qualified instructors. Unlike other branches of sailing where you can jump into a sailboat and learn as you go along, boardsailing requires a few key techniques which are better taught than picked up haphazardly by trial and error. Furthermore, it is always good to know exactly what is involved before you try it.

Balance By far the most important part of boardsailing is balance – the ability to make the board an extension of your legs and feet so that no matter what outside forces are acting on the body the board remains stable.

Many schools encourage newcomers to play around with the board minus its rig. It is in fact more unstable but this heightens the need to learn the correct way to clamber back on to the board and where to place the feet as you move around.

The Land Simulator If you attend a school in a temperate climate – i.e. the water is cold! – much of the initial teaching will be ashore using the land simulator, a simple device which enables a board to be mounted on a pivoting base. The simulator acts in much the same way as a floating board, enabling the instructor to give each pupil individual attention until the basic skills are mastered. Only then will you go afloat. Usually to a tethered board.

Basic Skills After learning how to climb on to the board the first thing to do is to align the board and rig so that the board is at right angles to the wind with the sail on the downwind side. This is referred to variously as the 'starting' or 'basic' position. It is the basis of all beginners' sailing.

Raising the Rig To sail you have to raise the rig from the water. This requires a carefully coordinated combination of balance and strength, especially with lightweight or unfit sailors. It is the one skill which must be mastered before you set out alone, and can become a safety consideration in strong winds when your strength is ebbing away.

Stand facing across the board with the front foot resting against the front edge of the mast step, and the back foot behind the mast. Bend the knees and reach forward to grasp the uphaul line as high up as you can reach. Bend

backwards using the weight of the body to unstick the sail from the water. Allow the water to drain away from the rig raising the mast slowly. When the sail has drained straighten up and pull the rig clear of the water by hauling hand over hand on the uphaul rope. Keep the board at right angles to the wind by varying the pull on the back or front hand. Once the sail is clear of the water it can be held with one hand and allowed to sway in the wind. Now the board is kept at right angles by swinging the sail to catch the wind.

Once you have learned to raise the rig from the leeward side you move on to rotating the board under the sail. After considerable practice you will begin to master the technique of placing your feet in the correct balancing position.

Finally, before you actually learn how to use the sail you must learn how to raise the rig from a windward position, as is the case when you fall backwards taking the rig with you. Set the board up at right angles to the wind with the mast pointing directly into the wind. Raise and drain the sail as before. As the wind gets under the sail pull the rig up quickly, moving around the front of the mast as the sail swings over the back of the board. Continue to move to the windward side of the board as the rig streams out to leeward. Points to watch are that the back of the board does not become lodged between the sail and the wishbone and that you keep opposite the sail as it swings across.

Sailing Once you have enough confidence to swing the sail about with one hand you can move on to bringing the sail to a starting position. Individuals soon develop their own techniques for this manoeuvre and schools vary on the degree of standardization they require of their pupils. The following method is simple and works!

1 Finish raising the rig with your back hand (hand nearest the back of the board) holding the uphaul close to the boom. Check that the board is still at right angles to the wind.

2 Start by gripping the wishbone, about 20 cm (8 in) aft of the mast, with the front hand crossing it over the back hand.

3 Releasing the uphaul pull the rig upright and swing the body so that you are looking at the front of the board.

4 Grasp the wishbone with the back hand so that the hands – now called 'mast' and 'sail' hands – are just in excess of shoulder width apart. Gently rake the mast forward with the mast hand so that you can see the front of the board through the sail window and pull the sail hand towards you until the wind begins to fill the sail and the board moves forward. After many unsuccessful attempts to maintain forward progress and to balance the pull of the sail you will begin to appreciate that the position of the rig – forwards, upright or backwards – determines whether the board turns away or towards the wind or sails a straight course.

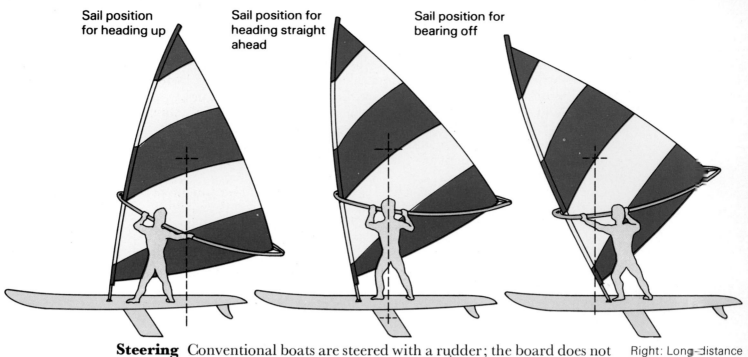

Sail position for heading up | Sail position for heading straight ahead | Sail position for bearing off

Steering Conventional boats are steered with a rudder; the board does not have one and must be controlled by raking the entire rig forwards or backwards so that the main drive of the sail is forward or behind the centre-board which is the pivotal point of the board. The illustration shows the effect of raking the rig.

POINTS OF SAILING

As you learn to sail closer to the wind you will find that the sail must be pulled in closer to the centreline – until you reach a point when you fall off backwards because that's as close to the wind as you can sail.

When the board is at right angles to the wind on a reach the sail is let out to a comfortable sailing position.

Sailing away from the wind the sail has to be set across the board; a difficult, unstable sailing position which requires considerable practice especially as the wind increases.

Manoeuvring Once you have learned how to steer towards and away from the wind by raking the rig fore and aft the next stage is to master the technique of making progress against the wind, which as the previous section shows, requires sailing craft to sail in a series of zig-zags towards a windward objective.

The change in direction through 90° is called *tacking* or *going about*. This requires the boardsailor to rake the rig aft to move the bow towards the wind, move around the front of the mast then reset the rig on the new tack. Again there are various ways of achieving a smooth tack; this one utilizes the uphaul and reflects the starting position we have already used.

Right: Long-distance sailing. A Sea Panther off the Cornish coast during a successful circumnavigation of the British Isles.

Racing: Reaching into the gybe mark.

Below: An expert gybing in strong winds. Note wake pattern throughout this sequence.
Sails at maximum speed on a reach.
Rakes rig forward to turn away from wind, banks board into turn; releases back hand.
Sail rotates quickly; boardsailor moves rapidly across board to maintain balance; back hand about to grasp boom.
Transfers body weight to boom to power away on new reaching course.

Tacking Start the turn towards the wind by raking the rig aft. As the board faces into the wind, move your body to keep it between the wind and the mast. Let the boom touch the water as you pull the sail in with the sail hand – this speeds the turn. Release the sail hand, placing it on the uphaul. As the board turns on to the new tack release the mast and grasp the uphaul close to the boom. Swing the rig to continue the turn until the board is at right angles to the wind. Grasp the wishbone with the mast hand, bring the rig to a sailing position and transfer the sail hand from the uphaul to the wishbone. Pull the sail hand to set the sail on the new tack. With practice, especially tacking from a reach to a reach, you will slowly develop your own technique.

Sailing Downwind Before you can gybe – change direction away from the wind – you have to master the technique of sailing downwind. Just turning away from the wind and having to stand behind the mast will take you some time. The ideal downwind sailing stance in light airs is to face forward with your feet level with the back edge of the centreboard housing. The rig must be plumb, i.e. it must not be raked towards the bow or the stern. It must be raked across the board so that the sail area is exactly divided by the centreline.

In stronger winds the whole rig is pulled towards the stern – you can even try sitting down holding the rig if the wind suddenly gets up and you have to sail downwind!

Gybing Once again, utilizing the downhaul for the transfer ensures that you are sailing downwind. Transfer the mast hand to the uphaul and release the sail hand. The sail will swing forward over the bow of the board: do not on any account let it touch the water. Grasp the wishbone with the new mast hand, lean the rig forward and to windward, release the uphaul and grasp the wishbone with your sail hand.

Preparing to sail. Note protective neoprene wetsuits and buoyancy aids.

SAFETY

Having looked at some of the basics of board handling it is important to remember that there is an element of danger in boardsailing, especially for the first-time sailor or weak swimmer.

Life Vest As a preliminary precaution wear a life vest – the waistcoat type – whilst you are familiarizing yourself with the board, then, when you become proficient, common sense or your local safety requirements will dictate what you wear.

Protective Clothing By far the most common form of protection in temperate climates is the neoprene wet suit which helps to maintain a normal body temperature in cold conditions. Some European water owners dictate the wearing of dry suits to prevent pollution of drinking supplies, and these suits are a must for extreme winter conditions.

In areas where water and air temperatures are above 70°F (21°C) the greatest need is to protect from sunburn until you have become acclimatized.

Exhaustion Cold and tiredness can rapidly lead to a situation where the boardsailor is no longer able to control, or even raise, the rig of his board. Outside assistance is essential and this can be summoned by smoke flares or by ensuring that you always sail with someone else. Exhaustion can quickly lead to hypothermia, a general loss of body core heat which, if not treated, results in death. Being aware of the dangers is half the battle, being prepared to accept the assistance of others is the other half.

Other Water Users Laws relating to rights of way exist at sea as well as on the highway. Know the Rules of the Road before going afloat. (See page 52.)

MORE ADVANCED BOARDSAILING

Once you have mastered the basic skills in winds below Force 3 you may need coaching to develop more advanced techniques to enable you to master stronger wind conditions. One of the first areas for improvement is to speed up your basic tacking and gybing manoeuvres and to concentrate on developing automatic responses to balance out the changing wind pressures on the sail.

Downwind Sailing Downwind sailing and gybing in stronger winds requires split second reactions based on a well proven technique. To acquire these skills you will have to seek help and advice from someone who is already skilled in these techniques.

Competitive Boardsailing One way of developing your skills is to involve yourself in some form of regular competition against other board-sailors. The simplest form is racing around a set course, usually triangular. All sailing racing is governed by the rules of the International Yacht Racing Union (IYRU). These are lengthy and complex. When you start you should know the basic right of way rules between sailing craft and you should have some idea of the nature of a race. Most courses do allow the competitor a variety of sailing points – beating, reaching and running – and it is wise to familiarize yourself with the course and any problems it may present before the race.

Take courage from the fact that everyone has to have a first race and that progress can be quite spectacular if you take the trouble to learn about the rules and the tactics of sailing the race course.

Freestyle or Tricks Sailing Because the board encourages individuality it is not surprising that many of the original boardsailors progressed to tricks sailing starting with leaning backwards until one's head 'dips' and progressing to somersaulting around one of the wishbone booms. There are various methods of supporting the rig either on the windward or leeward side of the sail.

One of the more spectacular tricks is to turn the board on its side. Rail-riding, as it is known, can then be used as the basis for even more ambitious tricks.

Slalom Courses Those who wish to develop ultimate boardhandling skills sail the slalom course in and out of a series of buoys laid parallel to the wind. The winner is the one with the fastest time or least faults upwind and back again.

Wave Jumping This has brought the sport back to its origins, the large breaking waves of the surfers. Wave jumping boards are shorter, have foot loops and multiple skegs. The principal aim of the wave jumper is to utilize waves to achieve take off and to fly as high and as fast as possible. Watch how others do it before borrowing a jumping board and trying for yourself!

Freestyle: Rail riding with reversed rig.

Above: Wave jumping. The feet are kept in position by footstraps. The sail acts as a wing prolonging the jump.

Below: Achieving lift-off in ordinary waves using a specialist jumping board.

FUTURE DEVELOPMENT

The final seal of approval was given to the sport when the International Olympic Committee accepted the Windglider Class for the 1984 Olympic Games. In addition, large international competitions are being sponsored by prestigious international companies, and if the sport can capture the imagination of the television companies, some of its more successful exponents will become superstars.

The sponsored competitions are breeding boardsailing professionals who travel around the world in much the same way as golfers, and this higher level of competition will encourage increasing numbers of boardsailors to enter area and regional events.